PORTABLE CHEF

Barbecue

& Salads for Summer

Jacqueline Bellefontaine

SMITHMARK

This edition published in 1998 by SMITHMARK Publishers,
a division of U.S. Media Holdings Inc.,
115 West 18th Street, New York, NY 10011.

SMITHMARK books are available for bulk purchase for sales promotion
and premium use. For details write or call the manager of special sales,
SMITHMARK Publishers, 115 West 18th Street, New York, NY 10011.

Produced by Haldane Mason, London

Acknowledgments
Art Director: Ron Samuels
Editorial Director: Sydney Francis
Managing Editor: Jo-Anne Cox
Editor: Ian Kearey
Design: dap ltd
Photography: St John Asprey
Home Economist: Jacqueline Bellefontaine

ISBN: 0-7651-0875-5

Printed in China

10 9 8 7 6 5 4 3 2 1

Note
Unless otherwise stated, milk is assumed to be full fat, eggs are medium,
and pepper is freshly ground black pepper.

The barbecues used for the photography in this book were kindly supplied by:
Weber, Yardley Road, Knowsley Industrial Park North, Kirkby, Liverpool, UK and
Castle Catering Supplies, 4 King James Court, London, UK.

Contents

Introduction

What is it that makes a meal cooked outdoors over burning coals so appetizing? Perhaps it's the fresh air, or the tantalizing aroma, or the sound of fresh food sizzling on the grill. Whatever it is, there is no doubt that barbecues are becoming more and more popular. This should be hardly surprising when you see just how many wonderful dishes can be cooked over charcoal. This book alone contains 120 recipes, leaving you with no shortage of inspiration.

Gone are the days when hamburgers were the staple of every barbecue party, although traditionalists will find recipes here for making fabulous burgers. But why not try fish, which cooks to perfection on the barbecue and is healthy too? There are also dozens of tasty marinades and bastes for meat lovers, as well as vegetarian dishes, salads, and side dishes. You can even cook a delicious dessert on the barbecue.

WHICH BARBECUE?

You do not need a large, sophisticated barbecue to produce mouthwatering food, although once you have tried some of these recipes you might want to invest in something larger.

Essentially, barbecues are an open fire with a rack set over the hot coals, on which the food is cooked. You can improvise a makeshift barbecue with nothing more complicated than a few house bricks and an old oven rack. Chicken wire and baking racks can also be utilized to cook on.

Conventional barbecues are, however, available in all shapes and sizes, ranging from small disposable trays to large wagon, gas-powered models.

As the names suggest, portable and semiportable barbecues tend to be small. Some types have a stand or folding legs; others have fixed legs. If you have a small model and are cooking for large numbers, cook the food in rotation so that guests can begin on the first course while the second batch is cooking.

Most brazier barbecues, which stand on long legs and have a windshield, are light and portable. On some models the height of the rack can be varied, and some types incorporate electrically powered rotisseries.

Covered barbecues are essential if you want to cook whole joints of meat. The lid completely covers the barbecue, increasing the temperature at which food cooks and acting, in effect, like an oven. The temperature is controlled by air vents. When used without the cover, these barbecues are treated like a traditional barbecue.

Wagon barbecues are larger, more sophisticated and quite expensive. They have wheels and often incorporate a tabletop.

Electric or gas barbecues heat volcanic lava coals. The flavor of dishes cooked on these is still good, because the flavor of barbecued food comes from the aromas of fat and juices burning on the coals, rather than the fuel itself.

EQUIPMENT

Apart from the barbecue itself, you do not need any special equipment, but do protect yourself with a pair of potholders. Long-handled tools can be useful, as well as being safer, and more convenient to use. They are not expensive, and if you cook on a barbecue regularly, it is a good idea to invest in a set. Racks for burgers, sausages, and fish are useful, but not essential.

You will need a set of skewers if you want to cook kabobs. Metal skewers should be flat to stop the food from slipping around as it cooks. Remember that metal skewers get very hot, so wear potholders or use tongs to turn them. Wooden skewers are much cheaper than metal skewers, but are not always very long lasting. Always soak wooden skewers in cold water for at least 30 minutes before use, because this will help to prevent them from burning on the barbecue, and then cover the exposed ends with small pieces of foil.

A water spray is useful for cooling down coals or dampening down flare-ups.

LIGHTING THE BARBECUE

Charcoal is the most popular fuel although you can use some wood. Charcoal is available as lump wood, which is irregular in shape and size, but easy to light, or as briquettes, which burn for longer and with a more uniform heat, but are harder to light.

Light the barbecue at least an hour before you want to start cooking. Stack the coals and use specially designed barbecue lighter fluid to help light the charcoal. Do not use household fire lighters because these will taint the food. Never use kerosene or gas to light a barbecue—both of these are very dangerous

if used incorrectly in this way and would not only taint the food, but could result in very serious injury.

The barbecue is ready to use when the flames have died down and the coals are covered with a thin layer of white ash. When the coals are sufficiently hot, spread them out into a uniform layer.

PREPARING TO COOK

Before you begin to cook, oil the rack so that the food does not stick to it. Do this away from the barbecue or the oil will flare up as it drips onto the coals. For most dishes, position the rack about 3 inches above the coals. Raise the rack if you want to slow down the cooking. If you cannot adjust the height of the rack, slow down the cooking by spreading out the coals or moving the food to the edges of the rack, where the heat will be less intense.

If your barbecue has air vents, utilize them to help you control the temperature—open the vents for more heat and close them when you need to reduce the cooking temperature.

It is very difficult to give exact times for cooking on a barbecue, so use the times given in the recipes in this book as guidelines only. You should always test the food, particularly pork, chicken, and meat on the bone, before serving, to make sure that it is cooked thoroughly.

Fish & Seafood

Fish tastes wonderful when it is cooked on the barbecue. This chapter is full of ideas, ranging from simple charbroiled whole fish to spicy marinated packets and kabobs. Oily fish is especially suitable for the barbecue because the flesh does not dry out over the direct heat. White fish will benefit from the addition of a baste or marinade if it is cooked directly over the coals, but smaller fish can be cooked whole, because the skin keeps in all the wonderful juices and acts as a natural protective coating. Barbecue fish steaks with a marinade or baste directly on the rack.

Choose a fish with a firm flesh or it may break up and drop on to the coals when you turn it. Alternatively, a hinged rack will make turning infinitely easier. A firm fish, such as monkfish, is essential for skewers, and wrap more delicate fish in kitchen foil, so that it cooks in its own juice.

Seafood does not need to be left in a marinade for long, making it ideal for impromptu barbecues. Shrimp Skewers, for example, can be made and cooked in minutes.

Indonesian-style Spicy Cod

Serves 4

INGREDIENTS

4 cod steaks	1 tsp grated fresh ginger root	salt and pepper
1 stalk lemon grass	$1/4$ tsp turmeric	red chilies, to garnish
1 small red onion, chopped	2 tbsp butter, cut into small	(optional)
3 cloves garlic, chopped	cubes	
2 fresh red chilies, seeded	8 tbsp canned coconut milk	
and chopped	2 tbsp lemon juice	

1 Rinse the cod steaks and pat them dry on absorbent paper towels.

2 Remove and discard the outer leaves from the lemon grass stalk and thinly slice the inner section.

3 Place the lemon grass, onion, garlic, chili, ginger, and turmeric in a food processor and blend until the ingredients are finely chopped. Season with salt and pepper to taste.

4 With the processor running, add the butter, coconut milk, and lemon juice and process until well blended.

5 Place the fish in a shallow, nonmetallic dish. Pour the coconut mixture on top and turn the fish until well coated.

6 If you have one, place the fish steaks in a hinged basket, which will make them easier to turn. Broil over hot coals for 15 minutes or until the fish is cooked through, turning once. Serve garnished with red chilies, if desired.

COOK'S TIP

If you prefer a milder flavor, omit the chilies altogether. For a hotter flavor do not remove the seeds from the chilies.

Blackened Fish

Serves 4

INGREDIENTS

4 white fish steaks	1 tsp freshly ground black	$^1/_2$ tsp salt
1 tbsp paprika	pepper	$^1/_4$ tsp ground allspice
1 tsp dried thyme	$^1/_2$ tsp freshly ground white	4 tbsp unsalted butter
1 tsp cayenne pepper	pepper	3 tbsp sunflower oil

1 Rinse the fish steaks and pat them dry with absorbent paper towels.

2 Mix together the paprika, thyme, cayenne pepper, black and white peppers, salt, and allspice in a shallow dish.

3 Place the butter and oil in a small saucepan and heat, stirring occasionally, until the butter melts.

4 Brush the butter mixture liberally all over the fish steaks, on both sides.

5 Dip the fish into the spicy mix until well coated on both sides.

6 Broil the fish over hot coals for about 10 minutes on each side, turning it over once. Continue to baste the fish with the remaining butter mixture during the remaining cooking time.

COOK'S TIP

Basting the fish with the butter mixture will ensure that the fish remains moist during cooking.

VARIATION

A whole fish—red mullet, for example—rather than steaks is also delicious cooked this way. The spicy seasoning can also be used to coat chicken portions, if you prefer.

Monkfish Skewers with Zucchini & Lemon

Serves 4

INGREDIENTS

1 pound monkfish tail	SAUCE:	salt
2 zucchini	4 tbsp olive oil	
1 lemon	2 tbsp lemon juice	TO SERVE:
12 cherry tomatoes	1 tsp chopped, fresh thyme	salad greens
8 bay leaves	$^1/_2$ tsp lemon pepper	fresh, crusty bread

1 Cut the monkfish into 2-inch chunks. Cut the zucchini into thick slices and the lemon into wedges.

2 Thread the monkfish chunks, zucchini slices, lemon wedges, tomatoes, and bay leaves onto 4 skewers.

3 To make the basting sauce, combine the oil, lemon juice, thyme, lemon pepper, and salt to taste in a small bowl.

4 Brush the basting sauce liberally all over the fish, lemon, tomatoes, and bay leaves on the skewers.

5 Cook the skewers on the barbecue for about 15 minutes, basting frequently with the sauce, until the fish is cooked through.

6 Serve the kabobs with salad greens and warm, fresh crusty bread.

VARIATION

Use flounder fillets instead of the monkfish, if you prefer. Allow two fillets per person, and skin and cut each fillet lengthwise into two. Roll up each piece and thread them onto the skewers.

Monkfish Skewers with Coconut & Cilantro

Serves 4

INGREDIENTS

1 pound monkfish tails	MARINADE:
8 ounces raw peeled shrimp	1 tsp sunflower oil
shredded coconut, toasted, to	$1/2$ small onion, finely grated
garnish (optional)	1 tsp fresh ginger root, grated
	$2/3$ cup canned coconut milk
	2 tbsp chopped, fresh cilantro

1 To make the marinade, heat the oil in a wok or saucepan and sauté the onion and ginger for 5 minutes, until just softened but not browned.

2 Add the coconut milk to the pan and bring to a boil. Boil rapidly for about 5 minutes, or until reduced to the consistency of light cream.

3 Remove the pan from the heat and allow to cool completely. Once cooled, stir in the chopped cilantro and pour into a shallow dish.

4 Cut the fish into bite-size chunks and stir gently into the coconut mixture, together with the shrimp. Chill in the refrigerator for 1–4 hours.

5 Thread the fish and shrimp onto skewers and discard any remaining marinade. Broil the skewers over hot coals for 10–15 minutes, turning frequently. Garnish with toasted coconut, if desired.

VARIATION

Look for uncooked shrimp in the freezer section in large supermarkets. If you cannot obtain them, you can use cooked shrimp, but remember they only need heating through.

Charred Tuna Steaks

Serves 4

INGREDIENTS

4 tuna steaks	1 tsp superfine sugar	TO GARNISH:
3 tbsp soy sauce	1 tbsp sunflower oil	parsley
1 tbsp Worcestershire sauce	salad greens, to serve	lemon wedges
1 tsp wholegrain mustard		

1 Place the tuna steaks in a shallow dish.

2 Mix together the soy sauce, Worcestershire sauce, mustard, sugar, and oil in a bowl. Pour the marinade over the tuna.

3 Gently turn the tuna steaks, using your fingers or a fork, so that they are well coated with the marinade.

4 Cover and place the tuna steaks in the refrigerator and chill for between 30 minutes and 2 hours.

5 Broil the marinated fish over hot coals for 10–15 minutes, turning once. Baste frequently with any of the marinade that is left in the dish.

6 Garnish with parsley and lemon wedges, and serve with salad greens.

COOK'S TIP

Tuna has a dark red flesh, which turns paler on cooking. Tuna has a good meaty texture, but if you are unable to obtain it, use swordfish steaks instead.

COOK'S TIP

If a marinade contains soy sauce, the marinating time should be limited, usually to 2 hours. If allowed to marinate for too long, the fish will dry out and become tough.

Charbroiled Bream

Serves 2

INGREDIENTS

2 small sea bream, scaled,
   gutted, trimmed, and
   cleaned
2 slices lemon
2 bay leaves
salt and pepper

BASTE:
4 tbsp olive oil
2 tbsp lemon juice
$1/2$ tsp chopped, fresh oregano
$1/2$ tsp chopped, fresh thyme

TO GARNISH:
fresh bay leaves
fresh thyme sprig
lemon wedges

1 Using a sharp knife, cut 2–3 deep slashes into the bodies of both fish in order to help them fully absorb the flavor of the basting sauce.

2 Place a slice of lemon and a bay leaf inside the cavity of each fish. Season inside the cavity with salt and pepper.

3 In a small bowl, mix together the ingredients for the baste using a fork. Alternatively, place the basting ingredients in a small screw-top jar and shake well to combine thoroughly.

4 Brush some of the baste liberally over the fish and place them on a rack over hot coals. Broil over hot coals for 20–30 minutes, turning and basting frequently.

5 Transfer the fish to a serving plate, garnish with fresh bay leaves, thyme, and lemon wedges, and serve.

VARIATION

If you prefer, use brill or a fish like gurnard instead of the sea bream.

COOK'S TIP

The flavor of the dish will be enhanced if you use good fresh ingredients in the sauce. Dried herbs can be used, but remember that the flavor is much more intense, so only use half the quantity of the fresh herbs listed above.

Salmon Yakitori

Serves 4

INGREDIENTS

12 ounces chunky salmon fillet	YAKITORI SAUCE:	5 tbsp dry white wine
8 baby leeks	5 tbsp light soy sauce	3 tbsp sweet sherry
	5 tbsp fish stock	1 clove garlic, crushed
	2 tbsp superfine sugar	

1 Skin the salmon and cut the flesh into 2-inch chunks. Trim the leeks and cut them into 2-inch lengths.

2 Thread the pieces of salmon and leek alternately onto 8 presoaked wooden skewers. Chill in the refrigerator until required.

3 To make the sauce, place all of the ingredients in a small pan and heat gently, stirring, until the sugar dissolves. Bring to a boil, then reduce the heat, and simmer for

2 minutes. Strain the sauce and leave to cool.

4 Pour about one-third of the sauce into a dish and then set aside to serve with the kabobs.

5 Brush plenty of the remaining sauce over the skewers and cook directly on the rack or, if preferred, place a sheet of greased foil on the rack and cook the salmon on that. Broil the skewers over hot coals for about 10 minutes, turning once. Baste the skewers frequently during cooking with the remaining

sauce to prevent the fish and vegetables from drying out.

6 Serve the kabobs with the dish of reserved sauce for dipping.

COOK'S TIP

Soak the wooden skewers in cold water for at least 30 minutes to prevent them from burning during cooking. You can make the kabobs and sauce several hours ahead of time. Refrigerate until required.

Salmon Brochettes

Serves 4

INGREDIENTS

1 pound salmon, skinned and cut into large chunks	1 green bell pepper, seeded and cut into chunks	1/4 cucumber, peeled, seeded, and chopped
1 tbsp cornstarch	4 tbsp olive oil	8 basil leaves
1/2 tsp salt	Italian bread, to serve	6 tbsp olive oil
1/2 tsp pepper		2 tbsp lemon juice
1 small egg white, beaten	TOMATO SAUCE:	salt and pepper
1 red bell pepper, seeded and cut into chunks	4 tomatoes, seeded and quartered	

1 Place the salmon in a shallow dish and sprinkle the cornstarch and salt and pepper on top. Add the beaten egg white and toss well to coat. Chill for 15 minutes.

2 Thread the pieces of salmon onto 4 skewers, alternating the fish pieces with the chunks of red and green bell peppers. Set the skewers aside while you make the tomato sauce.

3 To make the sauce, place all of the ingredients in a food processor and chop coarsely. Alternatively, chop the tomatoes, cucumber, and basil leaves by hand and mix with the oil, lemon juice, and seasoning. Let chill until required.

4 Broil the salmon brochettes over hot coals for 10 minutes, brushing frequently with olive oil to prevent them from drying out during the cooking time.

5 Slice the Italian bread at an angle to produce 4 long slices. Lightly toast on the barbecue.

6 Spread the sauce over each slice of bread and top with a salmon brochette. You can also serve the brochettes on toasted French baguettes.

Japanese-style Charbroiled Flounder

Serves 4

INGREDIENTS

4 small flounders	2 tbsp light brown sugar	TO GARNISH:
6 tbsp soy sauce	1 tsp fresh ginger root, grated	1 small carrot
2 tbsp sake or dry white wine	1 clove garlic, crushed	4 scallions
2 tbsp sesame oil		
1 tbsp lemon juice		

1 Rinse the fish and pat dry on absorbent paper towels. Cut a few slashes into both sides of each fish.

2 Mix together the soy sauce, sake or wine, oil, lemon juice, sugar, ginger, and garlic in a large, shallow dish.

3 Place the fish in the marinade and turn them over so that they are well coated on both sides. Let stand in the refrigerator for 1–6 hours.

4 Meanwhile, prepare the garnish. Using a sharp knife, cut the carrot into even-size thin sticks and clean and shred the scallions.

5 Broil the fish over hot coals for 10 minutes, turning them once.

6 Scatter the chopped scallions and sliced carrot over the fish and then transfer the fish to a warm serving dish. Serve immediately.

VARIATION

Use sole instead of the flounders, and scatter over some toasted sesame seeds instead of the carrot and scallions, if you prefer.

Smoky Fish Skewers

Serves 4

INGREDIENTS

12 ounces smoked cod fillet	MARINADE:	1/4 tsp dried dill
12 ounces cod fillet	4 tbsp sunflower oil	salt and pepper
8 large raw shrimp	2 tbsp lemon or lime juice	
8 bay leaves	rind of 1/2 lemon or lime,	
fresh dill, to garnish (optional)	grated	

1 Skin both types of cod and cut the flesh into bite-size pieces. Peel the shrimp, leaving the tail.

2 To make the marinade, combine the sunflower oil, lemon or lime juice, grated lemon or lime rind, dried dill, and salt and pepper to taste in a shallow, nonmetallic dish.

3 Place the prepared fish in the marinade and stir together until the fish is well coated on all sides. Marinate in the refrigerator for 1–4 hours.

4 Thread the fish onto 4 skewers, alternating the 2 types of cod with the shrimp and bay leaves.

5 Cover the rack with lightly buttered foil and place the fish skewers on top of the foil.

6 Broil the fish skewers over hot coals for 5–10 minutes, basting with any remaining marinade, turning once.

7 Garnish with fresh dill, if using, and serve immediately.

COOK'S TIP

Cod fillet is inclined to flake, so choose the thicker end which is easier to cut into chunky pieces. Line the rack with foil rather than cooking the fish directly on the rack so that, even if the fish does break away from the skewer, it is not wasted.

Apricot Charbroiled Mackerel

Serves 4

INGREDIENTS

4 mackerel	3 tbsp Worcestershire sauce	dash Tabasco sauce
14 ounce can apricots in natural juice	3 tbsp soy sauce	1 clove garlic, crushed (optional)
3 tbsp dark brown sugar	2 tbsp tomato paste	salt and pepper
	1 tsp ground ginger	

1 Clean and gut the mackerel, removing the heads if preferred. Place the fish in a shallow dish.

2 Drain the apricots, reserving the juice. Roughly chop half of the apricots and set aside.

3 Place the remaining apricots in a food processor with the sugar, Worcestershire sauce, soy sauce, tomato paste, ginger, Tabasco sauce, and garlic (if using) and process until smooth. Alternatively, chop the apricots and mix with the other ingredients until well combined.

4 Pour the sauce over the fish, turning them so that they are well coated on both sides. Chill in the refrigerator until required.

5 Transfer the mackerel to the barbecue either directly on the rack or on a piece of greased kitchen foil. Broil the mackerel over hot coals for 5–7 minutes, turning once.

6 Spoon any remaining marinade into a saucepan. Add the reserved chopped apricots and about half of the reserved apricot juice, and bring to a boil. Reduce the heat and simmer for 2 minutes.

7 Transfer the mackerel to warm serving plates and serve with the apricot sauce.

COOK'S TIP

Use a hinged rack if you have one, as it will make it much easier to turn the fish while it is cooking.

Mackerel with Lime & Cilantro

Serves 4

INGREDIENTS

4 small mackerel, trout, or
    sardines
$^1/_4$ tsp ground coriander
$^1/_4$ tsp ground cumin
4 sprigs fresh cilantro

3 tbsp chopped, fresh cilantro
1 red chili, seeded and
    chopped
grated rind and juice of 1 lime
2 tbsp sunflower oil
salt and pepper

1 lime, sliced, to garnish
chili flowers, to garnish
    (optional)
salad greens, to serve

1 To make the chili flowers (if using), cut the tip of a small chili lengthwise into thin strips, leaving the chili intact at the stem end. Remove the seeds and place in iced water until curled.

2 Clean and gut the mackerel, removing the heads if preferred. Transfer to a board.

3 Sprinkle the fish with the ground spices and salt and pepper to taste. Place a sprig of fresh cilantro inside the cavity of each fish.

4 Mix together the chopped cilantro, chili, lime rind and juice, and the oil in a small bowl. Brush the mixture liberally over the fish.

5 Place the fish in a hinged rack if you have one. Broil the fish over hot coals for 3–4 minutes on each side, turning once. Brush frequently with the remaining basting mixture.

6 Garnish with lime slices and chili flowers, if using, and serve with salad greens.

Mediterranean-style Sardines

Serves 4

INGREDIENTS

8–12 fresh sardines
8–12 sprigs of fresh thyme
3 tbsp lemon juice

4 tbsp olive oil
salt and pepper

TO GARNISH:
lemon wedges
tomato slices
fresh herbs

1 Clean and gut the fish if this has not already been done.

2 Remove the scales by rubbing the back of a knife from head to tail along the body. Wash and pat the sardines dry on absorbent paper towels.

3 Tuck a sprig of fresh thyme into the body of each sardine. Transfer the sardines to a large, non-metallic dish and season with salt and pepper.

4 Beat together the lemon juice and oil in a bowl and pour the mixture over the sardines. Let the sardines marinate in the refrigerator for about 30 minutes.

5 Remove the sardines from the marinade and place them in a hinged basket, if you have one, or on a rack. Broil the sardines over hot coals for 3–4 minutes on each side, basting frequently with any of the remaining marinade.

6 Serve the sardines garnished with lemon wedges, tomato slices, and fresh herbs.

COOK'S TIP

Look out for small sardines or sprats. Prepare them as above and use the same marinade. Place a piece of greased foil on the rack and cook over hot coals for 2–3 minutes on each side.

VARIATION

For a slightly different flavor and texture, toss the sardines in dried bread crumbs and then baste them with a little olive oil for a crispy coating.

Nutty Stuffed Trout

Serves 4

INGREDIENTS

4 medium trout, cleaned	rind of 1 orange, grated	oil for brushing
2 tbsp sunflower oil	2 tbsp orange juice	salt and pepper
1 small onion, finely chopped	1³/₄ cups fresh whole-	orange slices, to garnish
¹/₂ cup toasted mixed	wheat bread crumbs	orange and watercress salad,
nuts, chopped	1 medium egg, beaten	to serve

1 Season the trout inside and out with salt and pepper to taste.

2 To make the stuffing, heat the oil in a small saucepan and sauté the onion until soft. Remove from the heat and stir in the chopped nuts, grated orange rind, orange juice, and the bread crumbs. Add just enough beaten egg to bind the mixture together.

3 Divide the stuffing into 4 equal portions and spoon into the body of each fish.

4 Brush the fish liberally with oil and broil over medium hot coals for 10 minutes on each side, turning once. When the fish is cooked, the flesh will be white and firm and the skin will be beginning to crisp.

5 Transfer the fish to individual serving plates and garnish with orange slices.

6 Serve the fish with an orange and watercress salad and an orange and mustard dressing (see Cook's Tip).

COOK'S TIP

Serve the stuffed trout with an orange and watercress salad. For the dressing, mix together 2 tbsp orange juice, 1 tbsp white wine vinegar, 3 tbsp olive oil, ¹/₂ tsp wholegrain mustard, and salt and pepper to taste. Pour the dressing over the orange and watercress salad just before serving.

Barbecued Herrings with Lemon

Serves 4

INGREDIENTS

4 herrings, cleaned
4 bay leaves
salt

1 lemon, sliced
4 tbsp unsalted butter
2 tbsp chopped, fresh parsley

$^1/_2$ tsp lemon pepper
fresh crusty bread, to serve

1 Season the prepared herrings inside and out with freshly ground salt to taste.

2 Place a bay leaf inside the cavity of each fish.

3 Place 4 squares of foil on the counter and divide the lemon slices evenly among them. Place one fish on top of the lemon slices.

4 Beat the butter until softened, then mix in the parsley and lemon pepper. Dot the flavored butter liberally all over the fish.

5 Wrap the fish tightly in the foil and cook over medium hot coals for about 15–20 minutes, or until the fish is cooked through—the flesh should be white in color and firm to the touch (unwrap the foil to check, then wrap up the fish again).

6 Carefully transfer the wrapped fish packets to individual, warm serving plates.

7 Unwrap the foil parcels just before serving and serve the fish with fresh, crusty bread with which to mop up the deliciously flavored cooking juices.

VARIATION

For a main course use trout instead of herring. Cook for 20–30 minutes, until the flesh is firm to the touch and opaque.

Sardines with Olives & Tomatoes

Serves 4

INGREDIENTS

12 fresh sardines, gutted and
    cleaned
fresh basil leaves
4 plum tomatoes
8 pitted black olives

1 tbsp butter
1 tbsp olive oil
2 tbsp lemon juice
salt and pepper

TO GARNISH:
plum tomatoes, sliced
pitted olives, sliced
1 fresh basil sprig

1 Season the sardines inside and out with salt and pepper to taste. Insert 1–2 basil leaves inside the cavity of each fish. Using a sharp knife, make a few slashes in the body of each fish.

2 Cut the tomatoes and olives into slices and transfer to a large bowl. Tear 4 basil leaves into small pieces and toss together with the tomatoes and olives.

3 Divide the tomato and olive mixture among

4 large sheets of foil, and place 3 sardines on top of each portion.

4 Melt the butter and oil together in a small pan. Stir in the lemon juice and pour the mixture over.

5 Carefully wrap up the fish in the foil. Cook the fish over medium hot coals for 15–20 minutes until the fish is firm and cooked through.

6 Transfer the fish to individual serving plates and remove the foil.

Garnish the fish with slices of tomato and olive, and with a fresh sprig of basil. Serve at once.

COOK'S TIP

Slashing the body of the fish helps the flesh to absorb the flavors. It is particularly important if you do not have time to allow the fish to marinate before cooking.

Bacon & Scallop Skewers

Makes 4

INGREDIENTS

grated rind and juice of $1/2$
 lemon
4 tbsp sunflower oil
$1/2$ tsp dried dill

12 scallops
1 red bell pepper
1 green bell pepper

1 yellow bell pepper
6 slices bacon

1 Mix together the lemon rind and juice, sunflower oil, and dried dill in a nonmetallic dish. Add the scallops and mix thoroughly to coat in the marinade. Marinate for 1–2 hours in the refrigerator.

2 Cut the red, green, and yellow bell peppers in half and seed them. Cut the bell pepper halves into 1-inch pieces and then set aside in a small bowl until required.

3 Carefully stretch the bacon slices with the back of a knife blade, then cut each bacon slice in half.

4 Remove the scallops from the marinade, reserving any excess marinade. Wrap a piece of bacon around each scallop.

5 Thread the bacon-wrapped scallops onto skewers, alternating with the bell pepper pieces.

6 Broil the bacon and scallop skewers over hot coals for about 5 minutes, basting frequently with the lemon and oil marinade.

7 Transfer the bacon and scallop skewers to serving plates and serve at once.

VARIATION

Peel 4–8 raw shrimp and add them to the marinade with the scallops. Thread them onto the skewers alternately with the scallops and bell peppers.

Herrings with Orange Tarragon Stuffing

Serves 4

INGREDIENTS
---

1 orange
4 scallions
1 cup fresh whole-
    wheat bread crumbs
1 tbsp fresh tarragon, chopped

4 herrings, cleaned and
    gutted, or trout or sardines
salt and pepper
salad greens, to serve

TO GARNISH:
2 oranges
1 tbsp light brown sugar
1 tbsp olive oil
sprigs of fresh tarragon

---

1 To make the stuffing, grate the rind from half of the orange, using a zester.

2 Peel and chop all of the orange flesh on a plate in order to catch all of the juice.

3 Mix together the orange flesh, orange juice, orange rind, scallions, bread crumbs, and tarragon in a bowl. Season with salt and pepper to taste.

4 Divide the orange and tarragon stuffing into 4 equal portions and use it to fill the body cavities of the fish.

5 Place each fish onto a square of lightly greased kitchen foil and wrap the foil around the fish so that it is completely enclosed. Cook over hot coals for 20–30 minutes, until the fish are cooked through—the flesh should be white and firm to the touch.

6 Meanwhile, make the garnish. Peel and thickly slice the 2 oranges and sprinkle with the sugar. Just before the fish is cooked, drizzle a little oil over the orange slices and place them on the barbecue for about 5 minutes to heat through.

7 Transfer the fish to serving plates and garnish with the barbecued orange slices and sprigs of fresh tarragon. Serve with salad greens.

Caribbean Shrimp

Serves 4

INGREDIENTS

16 cooked tiger shrimp	MARINADE:
1 small pineapple	$2/3$ cup pineapple juice
flaked coconut, to garnish	2 tbsp white wine vinegar
(optional)	2 tbsp dark brown sugar
	2 tbsp shredded coconut

1 Peel the shrimp, leaving the tails attached if preferred.

2 Peel the pineapple and cut it in half lengthwise. Cut one pineapple half into wedges, then into chunks.

3 To make the marinade, mix together half of the pineapple juice and the vinegar, sugar, and coconut in a shallow, nonmetallic dish. Add the peeled shrimp and pineapple chunks and toss until well coated. Marinate for at least 30 minutes in the refrigerator.

4 Remove the pineapple and shrimp from the marinade and thread them onto skewers. Reserve the marinade.

5 Strain the marinade and place in a food processor. Roughly chop the remaining pineapple and add to the processor with the remaining pineapple juice. Process the pineapple for a few seconds in order to produce a thick sauce.

6 Pour the sauce into a small saucepan. Bring to a boil, then simmer for about 5 minutes. This can be done by the side of the barbecue if preferred.

7 Transfer the kabobs to the barbecue and brush with some of the sauce. Broil for about 5 minutes until the kabobs are piping hot. Turn the kabobs, brushing occasionally with the sauce. Serve with extra sauce, sprinkled with flaked coconut (if using), on the side.

Herb & Garlic Shrimp

Serves 4

INGREDIENTS

12 ounces raw shrimp, peeled
2 tbsp chopped, fresh parsley

4 tbsp lemon juice
2 tbsp olive oil
5 tbsp butter

2 cloves garlic, chopped
salt and pepper

1 Place the prepared shrimp in a shallow, nonmetallic dish with the parsley, lemon juice, and salt and pepper to taste. Stir gently to mix. Marinate the shrimp in the herb mixture for at least 30 minutes in the refrigerator.

2 Heat the oil and butter in a small pan, together with the garlic, until the butter melts. Stir to mix thoroughly.

3 Remove the shrimp from the marinade with a slotted spoon and add them to the pan containing the garlic butter.

Stir the shrimp into the garlic butter until well coated all over, then thread the shrimp onto several skewers.

4 Broil the kabobs over hot coals for 5–10 minutes, turning the skewers occasionally, until the shrimp turn pink and are cooked through. Generously brush the shrimp with the remaining garlic butter during the cooking time.

5 Transfer the herb and garlic shrimp kabobs to warm serving plates. Drizzle over any of the remaining garlic butter and serve at once.

VARIATION

If raw shrimp are unavailable, use cooked shrimp, but reduce the cooking time. Small cooked shrimp can also be cooked in a foil packet instead of on the skewers. Marinate and toss the cooked shrimp in the garlic butter, wrap in foil, and cook for about 5 minutes, shaking the packets once or twice.

Poultry

Poultry is a versatile food that can be cooked in a number of ways on the barbecue. Try it with herbs and garlic, tangy tomato glazes, or spicy Asian flavors. It also goes well with sweet glazes and fruit.

Chicken is ideal for the barbecue because the skin helps to keep the flesh succulent and gives a crispy coating. It is, however, essential that all poultry is cooked thoroughly. Test by piercing with a skewer in the thickest part—the juices should run clear when the meat is cooked. To avoid charred skins and raw centers, cook over coals that are not too hot. Place the rack about 4 inches above the coals. You should be able to hold your hand just above the rack for about 5 seconds; if it is too hot, reduce the temperature by raising the rack or spreading out the coals. However if the coals are not hot enough, the chicken will take too long to cook and will dry out.

Turkey can be a little dry, so baste it frequently with a glaze or marinade. Duckling has a stronger flavor and more fat than chicken or turkey. Larger joints of poultry can be par-cooked in boiling water, the oven, or microwave, and finished on the barbecue.

Jerk Chicken

Serves 4

INGREDIENTS

4 chicken portions
1 bunch scallions, trimmed
1–2 Scotch Bonnet chilies,
    seeded
1 garlic clove

2-inch piece fresh ginger root,
    peeled and roughly
    chopped
1/2 tsp dried thyme
1/2 tsp paprika
1/4 tsp ground allspice

pinch ground cinnamon
pinch ground cloves
4 tbsp white wine vinegar
3 tbsp light soy sauce
pepper

1 Rinse the chicken portions and pat them dry on absorbent paper towels. Place them in a shallow dish.

2 Place the scallions, chilies, garlic, ginger, thyme, paprika, allspice, cinnamon, cloves, white wine vinegar, light soy sauce, and pepper to taste in a food processor and process to make a smooth mixture.

3 Pour the spicy mixture over the chicken. Turn the chicken portions so that they are well coated in the marinade. Transfer the chicken to the refrigerator and leave to marinate for up to 24 hours.

4 Remove the chicken from the marinade and broil over medium hot coals for 30 minutes, turning the chicken over and basting occasionally with any remaining marinade, until it is cooked through.

5 Transfer the chicken portions to individual serving plates and serve at once.

COOK'S TIP

As Jamaican cuisine becomes increasingly popular, you will find jars of ready-made jerk marinade, which you can use when time is short. Allow the chicken to marinate for as long as possible for maximum flavor.

Favorite Barbecued Chicken

Serves 4

INGREDIENTS
---

8 chicken wings or 1 chicken
   cut into 8 portions
3 tbsp tomato paste

3 tbsp Pickapeppa sauce
1 tbsp white wine vinegar
1 tbsp clear honey

1 tbsp olive oil
1 clove garlic, crushed
   (optional)
salad greens, to serve

---

1 Remove the skin from the chicken if you want to reduce the fat in the dish.

2 To make the barbecue glaze, place the tomato paste, Pickapeppa sauce, white wine vinegar, honey, oil, and garlic in a small bowl. Stir all of the ingredients together until they are thoroughly blended.

3 Brush the barbecue glaze over the chicken and broil over hot coals for 15–20 minutes. Turn the chicken portions over occasionally and baste frequently with the barbecue glaze. If the chicken begins to blacken before it is cooked thoroughly, raise the barbecue rack if possible or move the chicken to a cooler part of the barbecue in order to slow down the cooking process.

4 Transfer the barbecued chicken to warm serving plates and serve immediately with fresh salad greens.

VARIATION

This barbecue glaze also makes a very good baste to brush over pork chops.

COOK'S TIP

When poultry is cooked over a very hot barbecue the heat immediately seals in all of the juices, leaving the meat succulent. For this reason you must make sure that the coals are hot enough before starting to cook.

Sticky Chicken Drumsticks

Serves 10

INGREDIENTS

10 chicken drumsticks
4 tbsp fine-cut orange
   marmalade

1 tbsp Worcestershire sauce
grated rind and juice of
   $^1/_2$ orange
salt and pepper

TO SERVE:
cherry tomatoes
salad greens

1 Using a sharp knife, make 2–3 slashes in the flesh of each chicken drumstick.

2 Bring a large saucepan of water to a boil and add the chicken drumsticks. Cover the pan, return to a boil, and cook for 5–10 minutes. Remove the chicken and drain thoroughly.

3 Meanwhile, make the baste. Place the orange marmalade, Worcestershire sauce, orange rind and juice, and salt and pepper to taste in a small saucepan.

Heat gently, stirring continuously, until the marmalade melts and all of the ingredients are well combined.

4 Generously brush the baste over the par-cooked chicken drumsticks and transfer them to the barbecue to complete cooking. Broil the drumsticks over hot coals for about 10 minutes, turning and basting frequently with the remaining baste.

5 Carefully thread 3 cherry tomatoes onto a

skewer and transfer to the barbecue for 1–2 minutes.

6 Transfer the sticky chicken drumsticks to warm serving plates. Serve with the cherry tomato skewers and a selection of fresh salad greens.

COOK'S TIP

Par-cooking the chicken is an ideal way of making sure that it is cooked through without becoming overcooked and burned on the outside.

Chicken Tikka

Makes 6

INGREDIENTS

4 skinless, boneless chicken
   breasts
$^1/_2$ tsp salt
4 tbsp lemon or lime juice

MARINADE:
$^2/_3$ cup unsweetened yogurt
2 cloves garlic, crushed

1-inch piece fresh ginger root,
   peeled and grated
1 tsp ground cumin
1 tsp chili powder
$^1/_2$ tsp ground coriander
$^1/_2$ tsp ground turmeric
oil or melted butter for
   brushing

SAUCE:
$^2/_3$ cup unsweetened yogurt
1 tsp mint sauce

1 Cut the chicken into 1-inch cubes. Sprinkle with the salt and the lemon or lime juice and let stand for about 10 minutes.

2 To make the marinade, combine the yogurt, garlic, ginger, and ground spices together in a small bowl until well mixed.

3 Thread the cubes of chicken onto skewers. Generously brush the marinade over the chicken.

Cover and marinate in the refrigerator for at least 2 hours, preferably overnight.

4 Broil the chicken skewers over hot coals, brushing with oil or butter and turning frequently, for about 15 minutes, or until cooked through.

5 Meanwhile, combine the yogurt and mint together to make the sauce. Serve the chicken tikka skewers with the mint and yogurt sauce.

VARIATION

Use the marinade to coat chicken portions, such as drumsticks, rather than cubes of chicken, if you prefer. Broil over medium hot coals for 30–40 minutes, until the juices run clear when the chicken is pierced with a skewer.

Indian Charred Chicken

Serves 4

INGREDIENTS

4 skinless, boneless chicken breasts	1/2 tsp ground cumin	CUCUMBER RAITA:
2 tbsp curry paste		1/4 cucumber
1 tbsp sunflower oil	TO SERVE:	salt
1 tbsp light brown sugar	nan bread	2/3 cup unsweetened yogurt
1 tsp ground ginger	salad greens	1/4 tsp chili powder

1 Place the chicken breasts between 2 sheets of baking parchment or plastic wrap. Pound them with the flat side of a meat mallet or with a rolling pin to flatten them.

2 Mix together the curry paste, oil, sugar, ginger, and cumin in a small bowl. Spread the mixture over both sides of the chicken and set aside until required.

3 To make the raita, peel the cucumber and scoop out the seeds with a spoon. Grate the cucumber flesh, sprinkle with salt, place in a strainer, and let stand for 10 minutes. Rinse off the salt and squeeze out any moisture by pressing the cucumber with the base of a glass or back of a spoon.

4 To make the raita, mix the cucumber with the yogurt and stir in the chili powder. Chill until required.

5 Transfer the chicken breasts to an oiled rack and broil over hot coals for about 10 minutes, turning once.

6 Warm the nan bread at the side of the barbecue. Serve the chicken with the nan bread and raita, and accompanied with fresh salad greens.

COOK'S TIP

Flattening the chicken breasts makes them thinner, so that they cook more quickly.

Cajun Spicy Chicken

Serves 4

INGREDIENTS

4 chicken portions	2 tsp cayenne pepper	4 tbsp sunflower oil
1 clove garlic	1 tsp dried oregano	2 tbsp lemon juice
1 tbsp light brown sugar	1 tsp dried sage	salt and pepper
3 tbsp paprika	1 tsp dried thyme	

1 Remove the skin from the chicken if you want to reduce the fat content. Using a sharp knife, make 2–3 slashes in the flesh of the chicken.

2 Cut the garlic clove in half and rub the cut surface over the chicken. Season the chicken portions with salt and pepper to taste.

3 Mix together the sugar, spices, and dried herbs in a small bowl. Sprinkle the mixture over the chicken and rub into the flesh. Cover and let stand in the refrigerator for at least 2 hours.

4 Mix together the oil and lemon juice in a small bowl. Brush the mixture liberally over the chicken.

5 Broil the chicken over medium hot coals for about 30 minutes, turning and basting occasionally with the oil and lemon mixture.

6 Check that the chicken is cooked by piercing the thickest part with a skewer—the juices should run clear. Return the chicken to the barbecue to cook for a little longer if necessary.

7 Transfer the chicken to warm serving plates and serve at once.

VARIATION

This recipe also works well with pork. Rub the spiced mixture onto pork chops or side pork slices—they will taste delicious.

Spatchcock Baby Chicken with Garlic & Herbs

Serves 2

INGREDIENTS

2 baby chickens, 1 pound each
6 tbsp butter
2 cloves garlic, crushed
2 tbsp chopped, mixed fresh
   herbs

BASTE:
4 tbsp olive oil
2 tbsp lemon juice
2 tbsp chopped, mixed herbs
salt and pepper

1 To open out each
chicken, place each
bird on its breast and use
sharp scissors or poultry
shears to cut along the
length of the backbone.
Open out the bird as much
as possible and place it
breast side up on a
chopping board. Press
down firmly on the breast
bone to break it.

2 Mix together the
butter, garlic, and
herbs until well combined.
Lift up the skin from the

breast of each chicken.
Divide the butter equally
between the 2 chickens and
spread over the breast
under the skin.

3 Open out each bird.
Thread 2 skewers
diagonally through each
bird to hold it flat.

4 Mix together the
ingredients for the
baste in a bowl.

5 Place the birds, bone
side down,

medium hot coals and
broil for 25 minutes,
basting with the lemon
and herb baste. Turn the
birds over and broil, skin
side down, for 15 minutes,
basting frequently, or until
cooked through.

COOK'S TIP

*Use a combination of fresh
herbs, thyme, rosemary,
mint, oregano, parsley, or
cilantro are all suitable.*

Sweet Maple Chicken

Serves 6

INGREDIENTS

2 boned chicken thighs
5 tbsp maple syrup
1 tbsp superfine sugar
grated rind and juice of
    $^1/_2$ orange
2 tbsp ketchup

2 tsp Worcestershire sauce

TO GARNISH:
slices of orange
sprig of parsley

TO SERVE:
Italian bread, such as focaccia
salad greens
cherry tomatoes, quartered

1 Using a sharp knife, make 2–3 slashes in the flesh of the chicken. Place the chicken in a shallow, nonmetallic dish.

2 To make the marinade, mix together the maple syrup, sugar, orange rind and juice, ketchup, and Worcestershire sauce in a small bowl.

3 Pour the marinade over the chicken, tossing the chicken to coat thoroughly. Cover and chill in the refrigerator.

4 Remove the chicken from the marinade— reserve the marinade.

5 Transfer the chicken to the barbecue and cook over hot coals for 20 minutes, turning the chicken and basting with the reserved marinade.

6 Transfer the chicken to serving plates and garnish with slices of orange and a sprig of parsley. Serve with Italian bread, fresh salad greens, and cherry tomatoes.

COOK'S TIP

If time is short, you can omit the marinating time. If you use chicken quarters, rather than the smaller thigh portions, parboil them for 10 minutes before brushing with the marinade and broiling on the barbecue.

Chicken Skewers with Lemon & Cilantro

Serves 4

INGREDIENTS

4 skinless, boneless chicken breasts
1 tsp ground coriander
2 tsp lemon juice

1 1/4 cups unsweetened yogurt
1 lemon
2 tbsp chopped, fresh cilantro
oil for brushing

salt and pepper

1 Cut the chicken into 1-inch pieces and place them in a shallow, nonmetallic dish.

2 Add the coriander, lemon juice, salt and pepper to taste, and 4 tbsp of the yogurt to the chicken and mix together until thoroughly combined. Cover and chill for at least 2 hours, preferably overnight.

3 To make the lemon yogurt, peel and finely chop the lemon, discarding any pits. Stir the lemon into the yogurt, with the cilantro. Chill in the refrigerator.

4 Thread the chicken pieces onto skewers. Brush the rack with oil and broil the chicken over hot coals for about 15 minutes, basting with the oil.

5 Transfer the chicken kabobs to warm serving plates and garnish with a sprig of fresh cilantro, lemon wedges, and fresh salad greens. Serve with the yogurt.

VARIATION

These kabobs are delicious served on a bed of blanched spinach, which has been seasoned with salt, pepper, and nutmeg.

COOK'S TIP

Prepare the chicken the day before it is needed so that it can marinate overnight.

Chicken Satay

Serves 4

INGREDIENTS

2 skinless, boneless chicken
    breasts

MARINADE:
4 tbsp sunflower oil
2 cloves garlic crushed
3 tbsp fresh, chopped cilantro
1 tbsp superfine sugar
$^1/_2$ tsp ground cumin

$^1/_2$ tsp ground coriander
1 tbsp soy sauce
1 red or green chili, seeded
salt and pepper

SAUCE:
2 tbsp sunflower oil
1 small onion, finely chopped

1 red or green chili, seeded
    and chopped
$^1/_2$ tsp ground coriander
$^1/_2$ tsp ground cumin
8 tbsp peanut butter
8 tbsp chicken stock or water
1 tbsp creamed coconut

1 Soak 8 wooden
skewers in a large,
shallow dish of cold water
for at least 30 minutes.
This process will prevent
the skewers from burning
during barbecuing.

2 Cut the chicken
breasts lengthwise into
8 long strips. Thread the
strips of chicken,
accordion-style, onto the
skewers and set aside while
you make the marinade.

3 Place the ingredients
for the marinade in a
food processor and process
until smooth.

4 Coat the chicken with
the marinade paste,
cover, and chill in the
refrigerator for at least
2 hours.

5 To make the sauce,
heat the oil in a small
pan and sauté the onion
and chili until they are

softened, but not browned.
Stir in the spices and cook
for 1 minute. Add the
remaining sauce
ingredients and cook the
mixture gently for
5 minutes. Keep warm at
the side of the barbecue.

6 Broil the chicken
skewers over hot coals
for about 10 minutes,
basting with any remaining
marinade. Serve with the
warm sauce.

Thai-style Chicken Skewers

Serves 4

INGREDIENTS

4 skinless, boneless chicken breasts
1 onion, peeled and cut into wedges
1 large red bell pepper, seeded

1 large yellow bell pepper seeded
12 kaffir lime leaves
2 tbsp sunflower oil
2 tbsp lime juice
tomato halves, to serve

MARINADE:
1 tbsp Thai red curry paste
2/3 cup canned coconut milk

1 To make the marinade, place the red curry paste in a small pan over medium heat and cook for 1 minute. Add half of the coconut milk to the pan and bring the mixture to a boil. Boil for 2–3 minutes, until the liquid has reduced by about two-thirds.

2 Remove the pan from the heat and stir in the remaining coconut milk. Set aside to cool.

3 Cut the chicken into 1-inch pieces. Stir the chicken into the cold marinade, cover, and chill for at least 2 hours.

4 Cut the onion into wedges and the bell peppers into 1-inch pieces.

5 Remove the chicken pieces from the marinade and thread them onto skewers, alternating the chicken with the vegetables and lime leaves.

6 Combine the oil and lime juice in a small bowl and brush the mixture over the kabobs. Broil the skewers over hot coals, turning and basting frequently with the oil and lime mixture, for 10–15 minutes, until the chicken is cooked through. Broil the tomato halves on the barbecue and serve with the chicken skewers.

Sesame Chicken Brochettes with Cranberry Sauce

Makes 8

INGREDIENTS

4 skinless, boneless chicken
  breasts
4 tbsp dry white wine
1 tbsp light brown sugar
2 tbsp sunflower oil
6¹/₂ tbsp sesame seeds

salt and pepper

TO SERVE:
boiled new potatoes
salad greens

SAUCE:
1¹/₂ cups cranberries
²/₃ cup cranberry juice drink
2 tbsp light brown sugar

1 Cut the chicken into 1-inch pieces. Stir together the wine, sugar, oil, and salt and pepper to taste in a large bowl. Add the chicken and toss to coat. Marinate in the refrigerator for at least 30 minutes, turning the chicken occasionally.

2 To make the sauce, place the ingredients in a small saucepan and bring slowly to a boil, stirring. Simmer gently for 5–10 minutes, until the cranberries are soft. Taste and add extra sugar if desired. Keep warm or chill, as required.

3 Remove the chicken pieces from the marinade with a slotted spoon. Thread the chicken pieces onto 8 skewers, spacing them slightly apart to ensure even cooking.

4 Broil on an oiled rack over hot coals for 4–5 minutes on each side, until just cooked. Brush several times with the marinade during cooking.

5 Remove the chicken skewers from the rack and roll in the sesame seeds. Return to the barbecue and cook for about 1 minute on each side or until the sesame seeds are toasted. Serve with the cranberry sauce, new potatoes, and fresh salad greens.

Chicken Skewers with Red Bell Pepper Sauce

Serves 4

INGREDIENTS

3 skinless, boneless chicken
   breasts
6 tbsp olive oil
4 tbsp lemon juice
1/2 small onion, grated
1 tbsp fresh, chopped sage
8 tbsp sage and onion stuffing
   mix

6 tbsp boiling water
2 green bell peppers, seeded

SAUCE:
1 tbsp olive oil
1 red bell pepper, seeded and
   finely chopped
1 small onion, finely chopped

pinch sugar
7 1/2 ounce can chopped
   tomatoes

1 Cut the chicken into even-size pieces. Mix the oil, lemon juice, onion, and sage and pour into a plastic bag. Add the chicken, seal the bag, and shake. Marinate in the refrigerator for at least 30 minutes, shaking occasionally. Place the stuffing mix in a bowl, add the water, and mix.

2 Cut each bell pepper into 6 strips, then blanch in boiling water for 3–4 minutes. Drain, rinse in cold water, then re-drain.

3 Form about 1 teaspoon of the stuffing mixture into a ball and roll it up in a strip of bell pepper. Repeat for the remaining stuffing mixture and bell pepper strips. Thread 3 bell pepper rolls onto each skewer alternately with pieces of chicken. Let chill.

4 Heat the oil and sauté the pepper and onion for 5 minutes. Add the sugar and tomatoes and simmer for 5 minutes. Set aside and keep warm.

5 Broil the skewers on an oiled rack over hot coals, basting frequently for about 15 minutes.

Maryland Chicken Kabobs

Makes 4

INGREDIENTS

8 chicken thighs, skinned and
boned
1 tbsp white wine vinegar
1 tbsp lemon juice
1 tbsp corn syrup or clear
honey

6 tbsp olive oil
1 clove garlic, crushed
4 slices bacon
2 bananas
salt and pepper

TO SERVE:
4 cooked corn cobs (see page
198)
mango chutney

1 Cut the chicken into bite-size pieces. Combine the vinegar, lemon juice, syrup or honey, oil, garlic, and salt and pepper to taste in a large bowl. Add the chicken pieces to the marinade and toss until the chicken is well coated. Cover and marinate in the refrigerator for 1–2 hours.

2 Stretch the bacon slices with the back of a knife and then cut each bacon slice in half. Cut the bananas into 1-inch lengths and brush them with lemon juice to prevent any discoloration.

3 Wrap a piece of bacon around each piece of banana.

4 Remove the chicken from the marinade, reserving the marinade for basting. Thread the chicken pieces, the bacon, and banana rolls alternately onto skewers.

5 Broil the kabobs over hot coals for about 8–10 minutes, until the chicken is completely cooked. Baste the kabobs with the reserved marinade and turn the skewers frequently. Serve with corn cobs and mango chutney.

VARIATION

For a quick Maryland-style dish, omit the marinating time and cook the chicken thighs over hot coals for about 20 minutes, basting with the marinade.

Turkey Steaks with Red Currant Glaze

Serves 4

INGREDIENTS

1/3 cup red currant jelly	1/4 tsp ground ginger	TO SERVE:
2 tbsp lime juice	pinch grated nutmeg	mixed salad greens
4 tbsp olive oil	4 turkey breast steaks	vinaigrette dressing
2 tbsp dry white wine	salt and pepper	1 Italian loaf
		cherry tomatoes

1 Put the red currant jelly and lime juice in a small pan and heat gently, stirring, until the jelly melts. Stir in the oil, wine, ginger, and nutmeg.

2 Place the turkey steaks in a shallow, nonmetallic dish and season with salt and pepper. Pour the redcurrant mixture on top, turning the meat so that it is well coated. Cover and chill in the refrigerator overnight.

3 Remove the turkey from the marinade,

reserving the marinade for basting, and broil on an oiled rack over hot coals for about 4 minutes on each side. Baste the turkey steaks frequently with the reserved marinade.

4 Meanwhile, toss the salad greens in the vinaigrette dressing. Cut the Italian loaf in half lengthwise and place, cut side down, at the side of the barbecue. Broil until golden.

5 Cut each half of bread into 4 pieces. Serve the turkey steaks on top of

salad greens and sandwiched between 2 pieces of bread.

VARIATION

Turkey and chicken escalopes are also ideal for cooking on the barbecue. Because they are thin, they cook through without burning on the outside. Leave them overnight in a marinade of your choice, or cook, basting with a little lemon juice and oil mixture, and season well.

Charbroiled Turkey with Cheesy Pockets

Serves 4

INGREDIENTS

4 turkey breast pieces, each about 8 ounces	4 sage leaves or ¹/₂ tsp dried sage	TO SERVE: garlic bread
4 portions full-fat cheese (Bel Paese, grated mozzarella, brie, or camembert), ¹/₂ ounce each	8 slices rindless fatty bacon 4 tbsp olive oil 2 tbsp lemon juice salt and pepper	salad greens cherry tomatoes

1 Cut a pocket into the side of each turkey breast. Open out each breast a little and season inside with salt and pepper.

2 Place a portion of cheese into each pocket, spreading it a little with a knife. Tuck a sage leaf into each pocket, or sprinkle with a little dried sage if you prefer.

3 Stretch the bacon out with the back of a knife. Wrap 2 pieces of bacon around each turkey breast, so that the pocket opening is completely covered. Use a toothpick to keep the turkey and bacon in place.

4 Mix together the oil and lemon juice in a small bowl until well combined.

5 Broil the turkey over medium hot coals for about 10 minutes on each side, basting with the oil and lemon mixture frequently.

6 Place the garlic bread at the side of the barbecue and toast lightly.

7 Transfer the turkey to warm serving plates. Serve with the toasted garlic bread, salad greens, and a few cherry tomatoes.

Spicy Turkey & Sausage Kabobs

Makes 8

INGREDIENTS

turkey breast fillet, about
  12 ounces
10 ½ ounces chorizo or other
  seasoned pork sausage
1 eating apple

1 tbsp lemon juice
8 bay leaves

BASTE:
6 tbsp olive oil

2 cloves garlic, crushed
1 red chili, seeded and
  chopped
salt and pepper

1 To make the baste, place the oil, garlic, chili, and salt and pepper to taste in a small screw-top jar and shake well to combine. Let stand for 1 hour for the garlic and chili to flavor the oil.

2 Cut the turkey into 1-inch pieces. Cut the sausage into 1-inch lengths.

3 Cut the apple into chunks and remove the core. Toss the apple in lemon juice to prevent discoloration.

4 Thread the turkey and sausage pieces onto 8 skewers, alternating with the apple chunks and bay leaves.

5 Broil the kabobs over hot coals for about 15 minutes, or until the turkey is thoroughly cooked. Turn the kabobs and baste them frequently with the flavored oil during the cooking time.

6 Transfer the kabobs to warm individual serving plates and serve at once.

COOK'S TIP

The flavored oil used in this recipe can be used to baste any broiled meat, fish, or vegetables. It will give plain foods a subtle chili flavor and will keep in the refrigerator for about 2 weeks.

Sherried Chicken Liver Brochettes

Serves 4

INGREDIENTS

14 ounces chicken liver,
    trimmed and cleaned
3 slices bacon
1 Italian loaf or small French
    bread
8 ounces baby spinach,
    washed

MARINADE:
$^2/_3$ cup dry sherry
4 tbsp olive oil
1 tsp wholegrain mustard
salt and pepper

MUSTARD MAYONNAISE:
8 tbsp mayonnaise
1 tsp wholegrain mustard

1 Cut the chicken liver into 2-inch pieces. To make the marinade, combine the sherry, oil, mustard, and salt and pepper to taste in a shallow dish. Add the chicken liver to the marinade and toss until well coated. Marinate in the refrigerator for 3–4 hours.

2 To make the mayonnaise, stir the mustard into the mayonnaise and chill in the refrigerator.

3 Stretch out the bacon with the back of a knife and cut each slice into 2. Remove the chicken liver from the marinade, reserving the marinade for basting. Wrap the bacon around half of the chicken liver pieces. Thread the bacon and chicken liver rolls and the plain chicken liver pieces alternately onto 6 pre-soaked wooden skewers.

4 Broil the skewers over hot coals for 10–12 minutes, turning and basting with the reserved marinade frequently.

5 Meanwhile, cut the bread into 6 pieces and toast the cut sides on the barbecue until they are golden brown.

6 To serve, top the toasted bread with spinach leaves and place the kabobs on top. Spoon the mustard mayonnaise on top and serve immediately.

Citrus Duckling Skewers

Serves 6

INGREDIENTS

3 skinless, boneless duckling
  breasts
1 small red onion, cut into
  wedges
1 small eggplant, cut into
  cubes

lime and lemon wedges, to
  garnish (optional)

MARINADE:
grated rind and juice of
  1 lemon
grated rind and juice of 1 lime

grated rind and juice of
  1 orange
1 clove garlic, crushed
1 tsp dried oregano
2 tbsp olive oil
dash of Tabasco sauce

1 Cut the duckling into bite-size pieces and place them in a nonmetallic bowl, together with the prepared red onion and eggplant cubes.

2 To make the marinade, place the lemon, lime and orange rinds and juices, garlic, oregano, oil, and Tabasco sauce in a screw-top jar and shake until well combined.

3 Pour the marinade over the duckling and vegetables and toss to coat. Marinate in the refrigerator for 30 minutes.

4 Remove the duckling and vegetables from the marinade, reserving the marinade for basting, and thread them onto skewers.

5 Broil the skewers on an oiled rack over medium hot coals, turning and basting frequently with the reserved marinade, for 15–20 minutes, until the meat is cooked through.

6 Transfer to a serving plate and serve the kabobs garnished with lemon and lime wedges for squeezing, if using.

COOK'S TIP

For more zing add 1 tsp of chili sauce to the marinade. The meat can be marinated for several hours, but marinate the vegetables for only 30 minutes.

Sesame Orange Duckling

Serves 4

INGREDIENTS

4 tbsp soy sauce
2 tbsp fine-cut marmalade
2 tbsp orange juice
2 cloves garlic, crushed

¹/₂-inch piece fresh ginger root, grated
1 tbsp sherry vinegar
4 duckling portions
2 oranges, sliced

4 tbsp sesame seeds

TO SERVE:
salad greens
fresh herbs

1 Mix together the soy sauce, marmalade, orange juice, garlic, ginger, and vinegar in a small bowl until well combined.

2 Trim away any excess fat from the duckling portions. Place the duckling portions in a shallow, nonmetallic dish and add the orange mixture. Cover and marinate in the refrigerator for at least 2 hours.

3 Divide most of the orange slices among 4 double-thickness pieces

of kitchen foil, reserving some orange slices to serve. Place a duckling portion on top of the oranges and pour some of the marinade over each portion. Fold over the foil to enclose the duckling completely.

4 Cook over hot coals for about 40 minutes or until the meat is just cooked through.

5 Remove the foil packets from the heat and sprinkle the skin of the duckling with the sesame seeds. Place the duckling,

skin side down, directly on the oiled rack over the hot coals and broil for a further 5 minutes, until the skin is crisp. Serve with the reserved orange slices, salad greens and fresh herbs.

COOK'S TIP

Cooking the duckling in foil packets retains all the flavor of the marinade. If you prefer, you can omit the foil and cook them directly on the rack. Turn and baste frequently until cooked.

Barbecued Duckling

Serves 4

INGREDIENTS

3 cloves garlic, crushed	1 tbsp chopped, fresh cilantro
2/3 cup light soy sauce	1 tsp five-spice powder
5 tbsp light brown sugar	4 duckling breasts
1-inch piece fresh ginger root, grated	sprig of fresh cilantro, to garnish

1 To make the marinade, mix together the garlic, soy sauce, sugar, grated ginger, chopped cilantro, and five-spice powder in a small bowl until well combined.

2 Place the duckling breasts in a shallow, nonmetallic dish and pour the marinade on top. Carefully turn the duckling breasts so that they are fully coated with the marinade on both sides.

3 Cover the bowl with plastic wrap and marinate in the refrigerator for 1–6 hours, turning the duckling once or twice so that the marinade is fully absorbed.

4 Remove the duckling from the marinade, reserving the marinade for basting.

5 Broil the duckling breasts over hot coals for about 20–30 minutes, turning and basting with the reserved marinade.

6 Cut the duckling into slices and transfer to warm serving plates. Serve garnished with a sprig of fresh cilantro.

COOK'S TIP

Duckling is quite a fatty meat, so there is no need to add oil to the marinade. However, you must remember to oil the barbecue rack to prevent the duckling from sticking to it. Do this well away from the barbecue to avoid any danger of a flare-up.

Glazed Duckling with Pineapple Salsa

Serves 4

INGREDIENTS

2 tbsp Dijon mustard
1 tsp paprika
$\frac{1}{2}$ tsp ground ginger
$\frac{1}{2}$ tsp ground nutmeg
2 tbsp dark brown sugar

2 duckling halves
salad greens, to serve

SALSA:
8 ounce can pineapple in
natural juice

2 tbsp dark brown sugar
1 small red onion, finely
chopped
1 red chili, seeded and
chopped

1 To make the salsa, drain the pineapple, reserving 2 tbsp of the juice. Finely chop the pineapple flesh.

2 Place the pineapple, reserved juice, sugar, onion, and chili in a bowl and mix well. Let stand for at least 1 hour for the flavors to develop fully.

3 Meanwhile, mix together the mustard, paprika, ginger, nutmeg, and sugar. Spread the mixture evenly over the skin of the duckling halves.

4 Broil the duckling, skin side up, over hot coals for about 30 minutes. Turn the duckling over and broil for 10–15 minutes, or until the duckling halves are cooked through.

5 Serve with fresh salad greens and the salsa.

COOK'S TIP

You could place the ducklings in a rectangular foil tray to protect the delicate flesh on the barbecue.

VARIATION

Use canned apricots or peaches to make the salsa for a tasty alternative. The salsa is also delicious served with pork, lamb, or chicken.

Meat

Most people think of meat when they think of barbecues, and even the simplest chop tastes wonderful when cooked on the barbecue. Add marinades or bastes, and you have the most appetizing meal you can possibly imagine.

The following recipes include suggestions for all of your favorite cuts of meat, as well as new approaches to those barbecue favorites, burgers and sausages. Don't be afraid of experimenting and mixing the bastes and marinades with different cuts and types of meat.

If you are having an impromptu barbecue, choose recipes with a baste, although, if time permits, marinating meat not only adds flavor, but helps to ensure that the meat is tender. Trim any excess fat from the meat so that it does not drip onto the coals, causing them to flare up—keep a water spray handy just in case.

Beef and lamb can be served pink in the center, but you must make sure that pork is cooked thoroughly. Test it with a skewer to see if the juices run clear.

Beef Toppers

Makes 6

INGREDIENTS

1 pound 9 ounces lean
    ground beef
1 onion, finely chopped
2 tbsp Worcestershire sauce
salt and pepper
sesame rolls, toasted, to serve

SAVORY MUSHROOMS:
2 cups sliced button
    mushrooms
1 tbsp soy sauce
1 tbsp Worcestershire sauce

GUACAMOLE:
1 avocado
1 clove garlic

1 tbsp lemon juice
1 tbsp tomato relish

BARBECUE SAUCE:
3 tbsp Pickapeppa sauce
3 tbsp ketchup
1 tsp wholegrain mustard
1 tbsp clear honey

1 Choose one or all of the following toppings. To make the savory mushrooms, combine all of the ingredients and set aside for at least 30 minutes.

2 To make the guacamole topping, peel, pit, and mash the avocado. Mix the avocado with the garlic, lemon juice, and tomato relish until well combined and

chill in the refrigerator until required.

3 To make the barbecue sauce, combine all of the ingredients and chill in the refrigerator until required.

4 To make the burgers, mix together the ground beef, onion, Worcestershire sauce, and salt and pepper to taste until well combined.

Divide into 6 portions and mold each into a neat patty, about 1/2 inch thick. Chill for at least 30 minutes.

5 Broil over hot coals for 5-10 minutes on each side. Serve the burgers in the rolls, with the topping spooned on top.

Beef Teriyaki

Serves 4

INGREDIENTS

1 pound extra thin beef steaks	SAUCE:	$1/2$ tsp ground cinnamon
8 scallions, trimmed and cut	1 tsp cornstarch	$1/2$ tsp ground ginger
into short lengths	2 tbsp dry sherry	
1 yellow bell pepper, seeded	2 tbsp white wine vinegar	
and cut into chunks	3 tbsp soy sauce	
salad greens, to serve	1 tbsp dark brown sugar	
	1 clove garlic, crushed	

1 Place the meat in a shallow, nonmetallic dish. Combine the cornstarch with the sherry, then stir in the remaining sauce ingredients. Pour the sauce over the meat and marinate in the refrigerator for at least 2 hours.

2 Remove the meat from the sauce and set aside. Pour the sauce into a small saucepan.

3 Cut the meat into thin strips and thread these, accordion-style, onto pre-soaked wooden skewers, alternating each strip of meat with the prepared pieces of yellow bell pepper and scallion.

4 Gently heat the sauce until it is just simmering, stirring it from time to time so that it does not stick to the bottom of the pan. Broil the kabobs over hot coals for 5–8 minutes, turning and basting the beef and vegetables occasionally with the reserved sauce.

5 Arrange the skewers on serving plates and pour the remaining sauce over the kabobs. Serve with salad greens.

COOK'S TIP

If you are short on time, omit the marinating, but the flavor will not permeate the meat as well.

Boozy Beef Steaks

Serves 4

INGREDIENTS

4 beef steaks	pepper	TO SERVE:
4 tbsp whiskey or brandy	fresh sprig of parsley, to	garlic bread
2 tbsp soy sauce	garnish	slices of tomato
1 tbsp dark brown sugar		

1 Make a few cuts in the edge of fat on each steak. This will stop the meat curling as it cooks.

2 Place the meat in a shallow, nonmetallic dish. Combine the whiskey or brandy, soy sauce, sugar, and pepper to taste, stirring until the sugar dissolves. Pour the mixture over the steak. Cover and marinate in the refrigerator for at least 2 hours.

3 Broil the meat over hot coals, searing the surface of the steak over the hottest part of the barbecue for about 2 minutes on each side.

4 Move the meat to an area of the barbecue with slightly less intense heat and cook for an additional 4–10 minutes on each side, depending on how well done you like your steaks. Test the meat is cooked by inserting the tip of a knife into it—the juices will run from red, when the meat is still rare, to clear, as it becomes well cooked.

5 Lightly barbecue the slices of tomato for 1–2 minutes.

6 Transfer the meat and the tomatoes to warm serving plates. Garnish with a sprig of fresh parsley and serve with garlic bread.

COOK'S TIP

Choose a good quality steak, such as fillet, club, T-bone, or porterhouse, with a light marbling of fat to prevent the meat from becoming too dry as it cooks. Quick-fry steaks can also be used, but these have to be pounded with a meat mallet to flatten and tenderize the meat.

Mexican Steaks with Avocado Salsa

Serves 4

INGREDIENTS

4 beef steaks
3 tbsp sunflower oil
1/2 red onion, grated
1 red chili, seeded and finely
  chopped
1 clove garlic, crushed
1 tbsp chopped, fresh cilantro
1/2 tsp dried oregano

1 tsp ground cumin

AVOCADO SALSA:
1 ripe avocado
grated rind and juice of 1 lime
1 tbsp sunflower oil
1/2 red onion, finely chopped

1 red chili, seeded and finely
  chopped
1 tbsp chopped, fresh cilantro
salt and pepper

1 Make a few cuts in the edge of fat around each steak to prevent the meat from curling as it cooks. Place the meat in a shallow, nonmetallic dish.

2 Mix the oil, onion, chili, garlic, cilantro, oregano, and cumin in a small bowl until well combined. Pour the marinade over the steaks, turning the meat so that it is well coated. Marinate in the refrigerator for 1–2 hours.

3 To make the salsa, halve the avocado and remove the pit. Peel and cut the flesh into small dice. Combine the avocado with the lime rind and juice, oil, onion, chili, cilantro, and salt and pepper to taste and mix well. Cover and chill in the refrigerator until required.

4 Broil the steaks on an oiled rack over hot coals for 6–12 minutes on each side.

5 Serve the steaks accompanied with the avocado salsa.

VARIATION

The avocado salsa can also be served with chicken. Reduce the amount of chili if you want a milder flavor. If fresh chilies are not available, look for jars of ground chilies, which are a good substitute.

Barbecue Steaks with Red Onion Marmalade

Serves 4

INGREDIENTS

4 beef loin steaks
2 tsp wholegrain mustard
2 tbsp sunflower oil
grated rind and juice of
$^1/_2$ orange
salt and pepper

cooked new potatoes, to serve

RED ONION MARMALADE:
2 tbsp olive oil
1 pound red onions, cut into
rings

$^3/_4$ cup red wine
rind of 1 orange, grated
1 tbsp superfine sugar

1 To make the marmalade, place the olive oil and onions in a saucepan and sauté gently for 5–10 minutes, until the onions are just softened and are beginning to turn golden-brown.

2 Add the wine, orange rind, and sugar to the pan and simmer for 10–15 minutes until the onions are tender and most of the liquid has evaporated. Let cool, then season.

3 Make a few cuts in the edge of fat around each steak to prevent the meat from curling as it cooks.

4 Using a knife, spread each steak with a little of the mustard and season with salt and pepper.

5 Mix together the oil and the orange juice and rind in a small bowl.

6 Broil the steaks over hot coals, searing the

meat over the hottest part of the barbecue for 2 minutes on each side, basting occasionally with the orange mixture. Move the meat to an area with slightly less intense heat and cook, basting occasionally, for 4–10 minutes on each side, depending on how well done you like your steaks.

7 Transfer to plates and serve with marmalade and new potatoes.

Surf & Turf Kabobs

Makes 6

INGREDIENTS

1 pound sirloin steak	MARINADE:	3 tbsp lemon juice
18 raw shrimp	5 tbsp oyster sauce	4 tbsp sunflower oil
	1 tbsp soy sauce	

1 Cut the steak into 24 even-size pieces and place in a nonmetallic dish.

2 Peel the shrimp, leaving the tails attached, as this makes them look attractive.

3 To make the marinade, combine the oyster sauce, soy sauce, lemon juice, and sunflower oil in a small bowl. Pour the mixture over the meat and marinate for 15 minutes.

4 Add the shrimp to the marinade, toss to coat, and marinate for 5 minutes.

5 Remove the meat and shrimp from the marinade, reserving the marinade for basting. Thread the meat onto metal or pre-soaked wooden skewers, alternating the steak with the shrimp. (Pre-soaking wooden skewers helps to prevent them from burning as the meat is cooking.)

6 Broil the kabobs over hot coals for 5–10 minutes, basting with the reserved marinade and turning frequently.

7 Transfer the "surf and turf" kabobs to warm serving plates and serve immediately.

VARIATION

Other shellfish, such as lobster and crab, can be added to the skewers. These kabobs are also delicious marinated in, and basted with, an herb, garlic, and oil marinade.

Beef, Tomato, & Olive Kabobs

Serves 8

INGREDIENTS

1 pound sirloin steak
16 cherry tomatoes
16 large green olives, pitted
Italian bread, to serve

BASTE:
4 tbsp olive oil
1 tbsp sherry vinegar

1 clove garlic, crushed
salt and freshly ground black
    pepper

FRESH TOMATO RELISH:
1 tbsp olive oil
1/2 red onion, finely chopped
1 clove garlic, chopped

6 plum tomatoes, seeded,
    skinned, and chopped
2 pitted green olives, sliced
1 tbsp chopped, fresh parsley
1 tbsp lemon juice

1 Trim any fat from the beef and cut the meat into 24 even-size pieces.

2 Thread the meat onto 8 skewers, alternating it with cherry tomatoes and olives.

3 To make the baste, combine the oil, vinegar, garlic, and salt and pepper to taste in a bowl.

4 To make the relish, heat the oil in a small pan and sauté the onion and garlic for 3–4 minutes, until softened. Add the tomatoes and olives and cook for 2–3 minutes, until the tomatoes are softened. Stir in the parsley and lemon juice and season with salt and pepper to taste. Set aside and keep warm or chill.

5 Broil the skewers on an oiled rack over hot coals for 5–10 minutes, basting and turning frequently. Serve with the tomato relish and slices of Italian bread.

COOK'S TIP

The kabobs, baste, and relish can be prepared several hours in advance, avoiding the need for any last-minute rush. For a simple meal, serve with crusty fresh bread and a mixed salad.

Beef with Mushrooms

Serves 4

INGREDIENTS

4 steaks, fillet or sirloin	5 1/2 ounces mixed exotic	TO SERVE:
4 tbsp butter	mushrooms	salad greens
1–2 cloves garlic, crushed	2 tbsp chopped, fresh parsley	cherry tomatoes, halved

1 Place the steaks on a chopping board and using a sharp knife, cut a pocket into the side of each steak.

2 To make the stuffing, heat the butter in a skillet, add the garlic, and sauté gently for about 1 minute.

3 Add the mushrooms to the skillet and sauté gently for 4–6 minutes until tender. Stir in the chopped parsley.

4 Divide the mushroom mixture into 4 and insert a portion into the pocket of each steak. Seal the pocket closed with a toothpick. If preparing ahead, allow the mixture to cool before stuffing the steaks.

5 Broil the steaks over hot coals, searing the meat over the hottest part of the barbecue for about 2 minutes on each side. Move the steaks to an area with slightly less intense heat and barbecue for a further 4–10 minutes on each side, depending on how well done you like your steaks.

6 Transfer the steaks to serving plates and remove the toothpicks. Serve with salad greens and cherry tomatoes.

COOK'S TIP

Exotic mushrooms, such as shiitake, oyster, and chanterelle, are now readily available in supermarkets. Look out for boxes of mixed exotic mushrooms, which are usually cheaper than buying the different types individually.

Meatball Brochettes

Makes 8

INGREDIENTS

1/8 cup cracked wheat	1 tbsp Pickapeppa sauce	oil, to baste
12 ounces lean ground beef	1 tbsp chopped, fresh parsley	8 hot dog buns, to serve
1 onion, very finely	beaten egg, to bind	
chopped (optional)	8 cherry tomatoes	
1 tbsp ketchup	8 button mushrooms	

1 Place the cracked wheat in a bowl and cover with boiling water. Leave to soak for 20 minutes, or until softened. Drain thoroughly and set aside to cool.

2 Place the wheat, ground beef, onion (if using), ketchup, Pickapeppa sauce, and parsley together in a mixing bowl and mix well. Add a little beaten egg if necessary to bind the mixture together.

3 Using your hands, shape the meat mixture into 18 even-size balls. Chill in the refrigerator for about 30 minutes.

4 Carefully thread the meatballs onto 8 presoaked wooden skewers, alternating them with the cherry tomatoes and button mushrooms.

5 Brush the kabobs with a little oil and broil over hot coals for about 10 minutes, turning occasionally and brushing with a little more oil if necessary.

6 Transfer the kabobs to warm serving plates. Cut open each of the hot dog buns and push the meat and vegetables off the skewers into the open rolls to serve, if you wish.

COOK'S TIP

The cracked wheat "stretches" the beef, making this a cheap and cheerful meal. It also produces a less dense meatball with a nutty texture that children often like.

Charbroiled Venison Steaks

Serves 4

INGREDIENTS

4 venison steaks	2 sprigs fresh thyme	TO SERVE:
$2/3$ cup red wine	1 bay leaf	baked potatoes
2 tbsp sunflower oil	1 tsp superfine sugar	salad greens and cherry
1 tbsp red wine vinegar	$1/2$ tsp mild mustard	tomatoes
1 onion, chopped	salt and pepper	
few sprigs fresh parsley		

1 Place the venison steaks in a shallow, nonmetallic dish.

2 Combine the wine, oil, wine vinegar, onion, fresh parsley, thyme, bay leaf, sugar, mustard, and salt and pepper to taste in a screw-top jar and shake vigorously until well combined. Alternatively, using a fork, whisk the ingredients together in a bowl.

3 Pour the marinade mixture over the venison, turn the steaks, cover, and marinate in the refrigerator overnight. Turn the steaks over in the mixture occasionally, so that the meat is well coated.

4 Broil the venison steaks over hot coals, searing the meat over the hottest part of the barbecue for about 2 minutes on each side.

5 Move the meat to an area with slightly less intense heat and barbecue for 4–10 minutes longer on each side, depending on how well done you like your steaks. Test if the meat is cooked by inserting the tip of a knife into the meat—the juices will run from red, when the meat is still rare, to clear, as the meat becomes well cooked.

6 Serve with baked potatoes, salad greens, and tomatoes.

Lamb Burgers with Mint & Pine Nuts

Serves 4

INGREDIENTS

1 pound lean ground lamb	2 tbsp chopped, fresh mint	TO SERVE:
1 small onion, finely chopped	salt and pepper	4 pita breads or soft rolls
1/4 cup pine nuts		1/8 cup feta cheese
		salad greens

1 Place the ground lamb, chopped onion, pine nuts, fresh mint, and salt and pepper to taste in a large bowl and mix together until all the ingredients are thoroughly combined.

2 Using your hands, divide the mixture into 4 and shape the portions into round burgers, pressing the mixture together well. Leave to chill in the refrigerator for about 30 minutes.

3 Broil the burgers over hot coals for 4–5 minutes on each side, turning once, until the juices run clear.

4 Warm the pita breads at the side of the barbecue or toast the rolls.

5 Crumble the feta cheese into small pieces and set aside until required.

6 Line the pita bread or rolls with the salad greens. Sandwich the burgers between the bread or rolls, and top with the crumbled feta cheese.

COOK'S TIP

If you do not have any fresh mint, use 1–2 teaspoons of mint sauce, which has a much fresher taste than dried mint. Chill the burgers in the refrigerator before cooking them, so that they become firmer and are far less likely to fall apart.

Butterfly Chops with Red Currant Glaze

Serves 4

INGREDIENTS

4 tbsp red currant jelly
2 tbsp raspberry vinegar
1/2 tsp dried rosemary
1 clove garlic, crushed

1 tbsp sunflower oil
4 butterfly lamb chops or 8
    loin lamb chops

4 baby eggplant
oil, for basting

---

1 To make the glaze, combine the red currant jelly, vinegar, rosemary, garlic, and oil in a small pan and heat, stirring occasionally, until the jelly melts and the ingredients are well blended.

2 Broil the chops over hot coals for 5 minutes on each side.

3 Cut each baby eggplant in half and brush the cut sides liberally with oil.

4 Broil the eggplant halves alongside the lamb for about 3–4 minutes on each side, or until completely cooked through. Set them aside and keep warm until required.

5 Brush the glaze over the chops and broil the meat for a further 5 minutes on each side, basting frequently, until the meat is cooked. Keep the red currant glaze warm at the side of the barbecue.

6 Transfer the lamb and eggplant to warm serving plates and pour the remaining red currant glaze on top. Serve at once.

VARIATION

You can use other lamb cuts for this dish—leg chops or rib chops are ideal. The red currant glaze also goes well with chicken; parboil or microwave chicken drumsticks, then brush them with the red currant glaze and finish off cooking on the barbecue.

Lamb with a Spice Crust

Serves 4

INGREDIENTS

1 tbsp olive oil
2 tbsp light muscovado sugar
2 tbsp wholegrain mustard
1 tbsp horseradish sauce

1 tbsp all-purpose flour
12 ounces neck slices of lamb
   or boned cushion shoulder
salt and pepper

TO SERVE:
coleslaw
slices of tomato

1 Combine the oil, sugar, mustard, horseradish sauce, flour, and salt and pepper to taste in a shallow, nonmetallic dish until they are mixed.

2 Roll the lamb in the spice mixture until well coated.

3 Lightly oil one or two pieces of foil or a large, double thickness of foil. Place the lamb on the foil and wrap it up so that the meat is enclosed.

4 Place the foil packet over hot coals for 30 minutes, turning the packet over occasionally.

5 Open the foil, spoon the cooking juices over the lamb, and continue to cook for a further 10-15 minutes, or until cooked through.

6 Transfer the lamb to a warm serving plate and remove the foil. Cut the lamb into thick slices and serve with coleslaw and a few slices of tomato.

COOK'S TIP

Lamb is naturally fatter than beef, which makes it a good choice for cooking on the barbecue.

COOK'S TIP

If preferred, the lamb can be completely removed from the foil for the second part of the cooking. Cook the lamb directly over the coals for a smokier barbecue flavor, basting with extra oil if necessary.

Kibbeh

Makes 8

INGREDIENTS

$^1/_2$ cup couscous
1 small onion
12 ounces lean ground lamb
$^1/_2$ tsp ground cinnamon

$^1/_4$ tsp cayenne
4 tsp ground allspice
salad greens and onion rings,
    to serve

BASTE:
2 tbsp sunflower oil
2 tbsp tomato ketchup

1 Place the couscous in a large bowl, cover with cold water and let stand for 30 minutes, or until the couscous has swelled and softened. Alternatively, soak the couscous according to the instructions on the packet.

2 Drain the couscous through a strainer and squeeze out as much moisture as you can.

3 Put the onion in a food processor and chop finely. Add the lamb and process briefly to chop the ground meat further.

Alternatively, grate the onion before mixing with the lamb.

4 Combine the couscous, lamb, and spices and mix well. Divide the mixture into 8 equal-size portions. Press and shape the mixture around 8 skewers, pressing the mixture together firmly so that it holds its shape. Chill in the refrigerator for 30 minutes.

5 To make the baste, mix the sunflower oil and tomato ketchup together until well combined.

6 Broil the kibbeh over hot coals for 10–15 minutes, turning and basting frequently. Serve immediately.

COOK'S TIP

Adding couscous to a ground meat mixture "stretches" the meat, making the dish very economical to make. You can also use this combination to make kabobs or burgers.

Barbecued Lamb Ribs

Serves 4

INGREDIENTS

breast of lamb, about 1 pound
    9 ounces
3 tbsp sweet chutney
4 tbsp ketchup
2 tbsp cider vinegar

2 tsp Worcestershire sauce
2 tsp mild mustard
1 tbsp light brown sugar

TO SERVE:
salad greens
cherry tomatoes

1 Using a sharp knife, cut between the ribs of the breast of lamb to divide it into slightly smaller pieces.

2 Bring a large saucepan of water to a boil, add the lamb and parboil for about 5 minutes. Remove the meat from the water and pat dry thoroughly with paper towels.

3 Combine the sweet chutney, ketchup, cider vinegar, Worcestershire sauce, mustard, and sugar in a shallow, nonmetallic dish to make a very smooth sauce.

4 Using a sharp knife, cut the lamb into individual ribs. Add the ribs to the sauce and toss until well coated.

5 Remove the ribs from the sauce, reserving the remaining sauce for basting.

6 Broil the ribs over hot coals for 10-15 minutes, turning and basting frequently with the reserved sauce.

7 Transfer the ribs to warm serving plates. Serve immediately with salad greens and cherry tomatoes.

VARIATION

Use side of pork strips if you prefer and, as with the lamb, parboil the pork to remove some of the excess fat from the meat.

Butterfly Lamb with Balsamic Vinegar & Mint

Serves 4

INGREDIENTS

boned leg of lamb, about
  4 pounds
8 tbsp balsamic vinegar
grated rind and juice of
  1 lemon

²/₃ cup sunflower oil
4 tbsp chopped, fresh mint
2 cloves garlic, crushed
2 tbsp light brown sugar
salt and pepper

TO SERVE:
broiled vegetables
salad greens

1 Open out the boned leg of lamb so that its shape resembles a butterfly. Thread 2–3 skewers through the meat.

2 Combine the balsamic vinegar, lemon rind and juice, oil, mint, garlic, sugar, and salt and pepper to taste in a nonmetallic dish that is large enough to hold the lamb.

3 Place the lamb in the dish and turn it over a few times so that the meat is coated on both sides with the marinade. Marinate in the refrigerator for at least 6 hours or preferably overnight, turning occasionally.

4 Remove the lamb from the marinade and reserve the liquid.

5 Place the rack about 6 inches above the coals and barbecue the lamb for about 30 minutes on each side, turning once and basting frequently.

6 Transfer the lamb to a chopping board and remove the skewers. Cut the lamb into slices across the grain and serve with broiled vegetables and crisp salad greens.

COOK'S TIP

If you prefer, cook the lamb for half the cooking time in a preheated oven at 350°F, then finish off cooking on the barbecue.

Red Wine Lamb Skewers

Makes 4

INGREDIENTS

1 pound lean lamb	MARINADE:	1 bay leaf
12 button onions or shallots	2/3 cup red wine	sprig of fresh thyme
12 button mushrooms	4 tbsp olive oil	2 sprigs fresh parsley
salad greens and cherry	2 tbsp brandy (optional)	
tomatoes, to serve	1 onion, sliced	

1 Carefully trim away any excess fat from the lamb. Cut the lamb into large pieces.

2 To make the marinade, combine the wine, oil, brandy (if using), onion, bay leaf, thyme, and parsley in a nonmetallic dish.

3 Add the meat to the dish and toss to coat the meat thoroughly in the marinade. Cover the dish and marinate the lamb in the refrigerator for at least 2 hours or preferably overnight.

4 Bring a saucepan of water to a rolling boil, drop in the unpeeled button onions, and blanch them for 3 minutes. Drain and rinse the onions under cold water, and then drain again thoroughly. Trim the onions and remove their skins, which will now slip off easily.

5 Remove the meat from the marinade, reserving the liquid for basting. Thread the meat onto skewers, alternating with the button onions and mushrooms.

6 Broil the kabobs over hot coals for 8–10 minutes, turning and basting the meat and vegetables with the reserved marinade a few times.

7 Transfer the lamb kabobs to a warm serving plate and serve with fresh salad greens and cherry tomatoes.

Moroccan Lamb Kabobs

Makes 4

INGREDIENTS

1 pound lean lamb
1 lemon
1 red onion
4 small zucchini
couscous, to serve (see Cook's Tip)

MARINADE:
grated rind and juice of
    1 lemon
2 tbsp olive oil
1 clove garlic, crushed
1 red chili, sliced (optional)

1 tsp ground cinnamon
1 tsp ground ginger
$1/2$ tsp ground cumin
$1/2$ tsp ground coriander

1 Cut the lamb into large, even chunks.

2 To make the marinade, combine the lemon rind and juice, oil, garlic, chili (if using), ground cinnamon, ginger, cumin, and coriander in a large nonmetallic dish.

3 Add the meat to the marinade, tossing to coat the meat completely. Cover and marinate in the refrigerator for a minimum of 2 hours or preferably overnight.

4 Cut the lemon into 8 pieces. Cut the onion into wedges, then separate each wedge into 2 pieces.

5 Using a canelle knife or potato peeler, cut thin strips of peel from the zucchini, then cut the zucchini into chunks.

6 Remove the meat from the marinade, reserving the liquid for basting. Thread the meat onto skewers alternating with the onion wedges, lemon pieces, and zucchini.

7 Broil over hot coals for 8–10 minutes, turning and basting with the reserved marinade.

COOK'S TIP

Serve these kabobs with couscous or tabouleh. Allowing $1/3$ cup couscous per person, soak the couscous in cold water for 20 minutes, until the grains have softened. Drain and steam for 10 minutes, or until hot.

Shish Kabobs

Makes 4

INGREDIENTS

1 pound lean lamb
1 red onion, cut into wedges
1 green bell pepper, seeded

MARINADE:
1 onion

4 tbsp olive oil
grated rind and juice of
   $^1/_2$ lemon
1 clove garlic, crushed
$^1/_2$ tsp dried oregano
$^1/_2$ tsp dried thyme

TO SERVE:
4 pita breads
few crisp lettuce leaves,
   shredded
2 tomatoes, sliced
chili sauce (optional)

1 Cut the lamb into large, even-size chunks.

2 To make the marinade, grate the onion or chop it very finely in a food processor. Remove the juice by squeezing the onion between two plates set over a small bowl to collect the juice.

3 Combine the onion juice with the remaining marinade ingredients in a nonmetallic dish and add

the meat. Toss the meat in the marinade, cover, and marinate in the refrigerator for at least 2 hours.

4 Divide the onion wedges into 2. Cut the bell peppers into chunks.

5 Remove the meat from the marinade, reserving the liquid for basting. Thread the meat onto skewers, alternating with the onion and bell peppers. Broil over hot coals for 8–10 minutes, turning and basting frequently.

6 Split the bread; fill with lettuce. Push the meat and vegetables off the skewers into the bread. Top with tomatoes.

VARIATION

These kabobs are delicious served with saffron-flavored rice. For easy saffron rice, simply use saffron stock cubes when cooking the rice.

Lamb Cutlets with Rosemary

Serves 4

INGREDIENTS

8 lamb cutlets
5 tbsp olive oil
2 tbsp lemon juice
1 clove garlic, crushed
1/2 tsp lemon pepper
salt
8 sprigs rosemary

baked potatoes, to serve

SALAD:
4 tomatoes, sliced
4 scallions, sliced diagonally

DRESSING:
2 tbsp olive oil
1 tbsp lemon juice
1 clove garlic, chopped
1/4 tsp fresh rosemary, finely
  chopped

1 Trim the lamb cutlets by cutting away the flesh with a sharp knife to expose the tips of the bones.

2 Place the olive oil, lemon juice, garlic, lemon pepper, and salt in a shallow, nonmetallic dish and whisk with a fork to combine.

3 Lay the sprigs of rosemary in the dish and place the lamb on top. Marinate for at least 1 hour in the refrigerator, turning the cutlets once.

4 Remove the cutlets from the marinade and wrap a little foil around the bones to stop them from burning.

5 Place the sprigs of rosemary on the rack and place the lamb on top. Broil for about 10–15 minutes, turning once.

6 Meanwhile, make the salad and dressing.

Arrange the tomatoes on a serving dish and scatter the scallions on top. Place all the ingredients for the dressing in a screw-top jar, shake well, and pour over the salad. Serve with the broiled lamb cutlets and baked potatoes.

Lamb with Mango & Chili

Serves 4

INGREDIENTS

4 loin of lamb or English chops

4 tbsp mango chutney

2 tsp chili sauce

broiled vegetables, to serve

SPICY MANGO RELISH:

1 ripe mango

2 tbsp cider vinegar

2 tbsp light brown sugar

$1/2$ tsp ground cinnamon

$1/2$ tsp ground ginger

1 To make the spicy mango relish, cut the mango lengthwise down both sides of the large, flat pit and discard the pit. Peel the mango and cut the flesh into even-size chunks.

2 Place the cider vinegar, sugar, cinnamon, and ginger in a small pan and heat gently, stirring continuously, until the sugar has completely dissolved.

3 Stir the mango into the mixture in the pan and cook gently at the side of

the barbecue for about 5 minutes, or until the mango is soft.

4 Barbecue the chops on an oiled rack for about 4 minutes on each side.

5 Combine the mango chutney and chili sauce in a small bowl and brush the glaze over both sides of the chops.

6 Continue to barbecue for a further 2–5 minutes on each side, until the lamb is cooked, turning and basting frequently with the chutney and chili glaze.

7 Serve the lamb with a selection of broiled vegetables and the spicy mango relish.

VARIATION

The spicy mango relish can also be served cold. Simmer the combined ingredients for 5 minutes, then remove from the heat and allow to cool. Chill in the refrigerator until required. You can also use the mango chutney and chili glaze on other cuts of lamb or on pork chops.

Indian Kofta

Makes 8

INGREDIENTS

1 small onion
1 pound minced lamb
2 tbsp curry paste
2 tbsp unsweetened yogurt
oil, to baste
sprigs of fresh cilantro,
    to garnish

TOMATO SAMBAL:
3 tomatoes, seeded and diced
pinch of ground coriander
pinch of ground cumin
2 tsp chopped, fresh cilantro
salt and pepper

TO SERVE:
poppadam
chutney

1 Put the onion in a food processor and chop finely. Add the lamb and process briefly to chop the ground meat further. Chopping the lamb again will help the meat mixture to hold together during cooking. If you do not have a food processor, grate the onion finely before mixing it with the ground lamb.

2 Add the curry paste and yogurt and mix well. Divide the mixture into 8 equal portions.

3 Press and shape the mixture into 8 sausage shapes and push each one onto a skewer, pressing the mixture together firmly so that it holds its shape. Chill the kabobs for at least 30 minutes or until required.

4 To make the tomato sambal, mix together the tomatoes, coriander, cumin, chopped cilantro, and salt and pepper to taste in a bowl. Let stand for at least 30 minutes for the flavors to combine.

5 Broil the kabobs on an oiled rack over hot coals for 10–15 minutes, turning frequently. Baste the kabobs with a little oil if required.

6 Transfer to serving plates and garnish with fresh cilantro. Serve accompanied with poppadam, chutney, and the tomato sambal.

Sweet Lamb Fillet

Serves 4

INGREDIENTS

2 fillets of lamb, 8 ounces
    each
1 tbsp olive oil
1/2 onion, finely chopped
1 clove garlic, crushed
1-inch piece fresh ginger root,
    grated

5 tbsp apple juice
3 tbsp smooth apple sauce
1 tbsp light brown sugar
1 tbsp ketchup
1/2 tsp mild mustard
salt and pepper

salad greens, croutons, and
    fresh crusty bread, to serve

1 Place the lamb fillets on a large piece of double thickness foil. Season with salt and pepper to taste.

2 Heat the oil in a small pan and sauté the onion and garlic for 2–3 minutes, until softened, but not browned. Stir in the grated ginger and cook for 1 minute, stirring occasionally.

3 Stir in the apple juice, apple sauce, sugar, ketchup, and mustard and bring to a boil. Boil rapidly for about 10 minutes, until reduced by half. Stir the mixture occasionally so that it does not burn and stick to the pan.

4 Brush half of the sauce over the lamb, then wrap up the lamb in the foil to completely enclose it. Cook the lamb over hot coals for about 25 minutes, turning the packet over from time to time so that it cooks thoroughly.

5 Open the foil packets and brush the lamb with some of the sauce. Continue to barbecue for another 15–20 minutes, or until cooked through and tender.

6 Place the lamb on a chopping board, remove the foil, and cut into thick slices. Transfer to serving plates and spoon the remaining sauce on top. Serve with salad greens, croutons, and fresh crusty bread.

Lamb Noisettes with Tomato Salsa

Serves 4

INGREDIENTS

8 lamb noisettes	sprig of fresh basil, to garnish	8 stuffed green olives
4 basil leaves	salad greens, to serve	1 tbsp lime juice
2 tbsp olive oil		pinch of superfine sugar
grated rind and juice of	SALSA:	
½ lime	6 tomatoes	
salt and pepper	4 basil leaves	

1 Place the lamb noisettes in a shallow, nonmetallic dish. Tear the basil leaves into small pieces and scatter them over the lamb.

2 Drizzle the oil and lime juice over the lamb and add the lime rind. Season with salt and pepper to taste. Cover and marinate in the refrigerator for at least 1 hour or preferably overnight.

3 To make the salsa, skin the tomatoes by cutting a small cross at the stem. Drop the tomatoes into boiling water for about 30 seconds, remove with a slotted spoon, and then peel off the skins.

4 Cut the tomatoes in half, then scoop out the seeds, and discard them. Cut the tomato flesh into large dice. Tear the basil leaves into pieces. Chop the olives. Mix together the tomatoes, basil, olives, lime juice, and sugar in a bowl and set aside for at least 1 hour or until required.

5 Remove the lamb from the marinade, reserving the marinade for basting. Broil over hot coals for 10–15 minutes, turning once and basting with the marinade.

6 Garnish with a sprig of basil and serve with the tomato salsa and salad greens.

Caribbean Pork

Serves 4

INGREDIENTS

4 pork loin chops
4 tbsp dark brown sugar
4 tbsp orange or pineapple
  juice
2 tbsp Jamaican rum
1 tbsp shredded coconut
1/2 tsp ground cinnamon
mixed salad greens, to serve

COCONUT RICE:
1 generous cup Basmati rice
2 cups water
2/3 cup coconut milk
4 tbsp raisins
4 tbsp roasted peanuts or
  cashew nuts
salt and pepper

2 tbsp shredded coconut,
  toasted

1 Trim any excess fat from the pork and place the chops in a shallow, nonmetallic dish.

2 Combine the sugar, fruit juice, rum, coconut, and cinnamon in a bowl, stirring until the sugar dissolves. Pour the mixture over the pork and marinate in the refrigerator for at least 2 hours.

3 Remove the pork from the marinade,

reserving the liquid for basting. Broil over hot coals for 15–20 minutes, basting with the marinade.

4 Meanwhile, make the coconut rice. Rinse the rice under cold water, place it in a pan with the water and coconut milk, and bring gently to a boil. Stir, cover, and reduce the heat. Simmer for 12 minutes, or until the rice is tender and the liquid has been absorbed. Fluff up with a fork.

5 Stir the raisins and nuts into the rice, season with salt and pepper to taste, and sprinkle with the coconut. Transfer the pork and rice to warm serving plates and serve with the mixed salad greens.

Ham Steaks with Spicy Apple Rings

Serves 4

INGREDIENTS

4 ham steaks, about 6 ounces each	1 tbsp sunflower oil	$^1/_4$ tsp ground nutmeg
1–2 tsp wholegrain mustard	APPLE RINGS:	$^1/_4$ tsp ground cinnamon
1 tbsp honey	2 green eating apples	$^1/_4$ tsp ground allspice
2 tbsp lemon juice	2 tsp raw sugar	1–2 tbsp melted butter

1 Using a pair of scissors, make a few cuts around the edges of the ham steaks to prevent them from curling up as they cook. Spread a little wholegrain mustard over the steaks.

2 Mix the honey, lemon juice, and sunflower oil in a bowl until well combined.

3 To prepare the apple rings, core the apples and cut them into thick slices. Mix the sugar with the spices and press the apple slices in the mixture until well coated on both sides.

4 Broil the steaks over hot coals for 3–4 minutes on each side, basting with the honey and lemon mixture to prevent the meat from drying out during cooking.

5 Brush the apple slices with a little melted butter and broil alongside the meat for about 3–4 minutes, turning once and brushing with melted butter as they cook.

6 Serve with the apple slices as a garnish.

COOK'S TIP

If you have time, soak the steaks in cold water for 30–60 minutes before cooking—this process will remove the excess salt.

Pork & Apple Skewers with Mustard

Makes 4

INGREDIENTS

1 pound pork tenderloin
2 eating apples
a little lemon juice
1 lemon
2 tsp wholegrain mustard

2 tsp Dijon mustard
2 tbsp apple or orange juice
2 tbsp sunflower oil
crusty brown bread, to serve

MUSTARD SAUCE:
1 tbsp wholegrain mustard
1 tsp Dijon mustard
6 tbsp light cream

1 To make the mustard sauce, combine the wholegrain and Dijon mustards in a bowl and blend in the cream. Set aside while you prepare the pork and apple skewers.

2 Cut the pork tenderloin into bite-size pieces and set aside.

3 Core the apples, then cut them into thick wedges. Toss the apple wedges in a little lemon juice—this will prevent any discoloration. Cut the lemon into slices.

4 Thread the pork, apple, and lemon slices alternately onto 4 skewers.

5 Mix together the mustards, fruit juice, and oil in a bowl until well combined. Brush the mixture over the kabobs and broil over hot coals for 10–15 minutes, turning and basting frequently with the mustard marinade.

6 Transfer the kabobs to warm serving plates and spoon a little of the mustard sauce on top. Serve hot.

COOK'S TIP

There are many varieties of mustard available, including English, which is very hot, Dijon, which is milder, and wholegrain, which contains whole mustard seeds. Mustards flavored with other ingredients, such as honey or chili, are also available.

Pork Ribs with Plum Sauce

Serves 4–6

INGREDIENTS

2 pounds pork spareribs	1-inch piece fresh ginger root,	2 tbsp soy sauce
2 tbsp sunflower oil	grated	4–6 scallions, to garnish
1 tsp sesame oil	²/₃ cup plum sauce	(optional)
2 cloves garlic, crushed	2 tbsp dry sherry	
	2 tbsp hoisin sauce	

1 To prepare the garnish, trim the scallions to about 3 inches long. Slice both ends into thin strips, leaving the onion intact in the center.

2 Put the scallions into a bowl of iced water for at least 30 minutes, until the ends start to curl up. Leave them in the water and set aside until required for the garnish.

3 If you buy the spareribs in a single piece, cut them into individual ribs. Bring a large pan of water to a boil and add the ribs. Cook for 5 minutes, then drain them thoroughly.

4 Heat the oils together in a pan, add the garlic and ginger, and cook gently for 1–2 minutes to bring out the flavor. Stir in the plum sauce, sherry, hoisin sauce, and soy sauce and heat gently until warmed through.

5 Brush the sauce over the pork ribs. Broil over hot coals for 5–10 minutes, then move the ribs to a cooler part of the barbecue. Broil for a further 15–20 minutes, basting with the remaining sauce. Transfer to warm serving plates, garnish with the scallion brushes, and serve hot.

COOK'S TIP

Parboiling the ribs removes excess fat, which helps prevent the ribs from splitting during cooking. Do not be put off by the large quantity—there is only a little meat on each, but they are quite cheap to buy.

Fruity Pork Skewers

Makes 4

INGREDIENTS

4 boneless pork loin steaks	slices of orange and lemon,	MARINADE:
8 ready-to-eat prunes	to garnish	4 tbsp orange juice
8 ready-to-eat dried apricots		2 tbsp olive oil
4 bay leaves		1 tsp ground bay leaves
		salt and pepper

1 Trim the visible fat from the pork and cut the meat into even-size chunks.

2 Place the pork in a shallow, nonmetallic dish and add the prunes and apricots.

3 To make the marinade, mix together the orange juice, oil, bay leaves, and salt and pepper to taste in a bowl.

4 Pour the marinade over the pork and fruit and toss until well coated.

Marinate in the refrigerator for at least 1 hour or preferably overnight.

5 Soak 4 wooden skewers in cold water to prevent them from catching fire on the barbecue during cooking.

6 Remove the pork and fruit from the marinade, using a slotted spoon, reserving the marinade for basting. Thread the pork and fruit onto the skewers, alternating with the bay leaves.

7 Broil the skewers on an oiled rack over medium hot coals for 10–15 minutes, turning and frequently basting with the reserved marinade, or until the pork is cooked through.

8 Transfer the pork and fruit skewers to warm serving plates. Garnish with slices of orange and lemon and serve hot.

Spicy Pork Ribs

Serves 4–6

INGREDIENTS

2 pounds pork spareribs	1 clove garlic, crushed	red chilies, to garnish
2/3 cup sieved tomatoes	1 tsp dried thyme	(optional)
2 tbsp red wine vinegar	1/2 tsp dried rosemary	mixed salad greens, to serve
2 tbsp dark brown sugar	1 tsp chili sauce	

1 If you buy the spareribs in a single piece, carefully cut them into individual ribs using a very sharp knife.

2 Bring a large saucepan of water to a boil and add the pork ribs. Cook the ribs for 10 minutes, then drain them thoroughly. Place the ribs in a large, shallow, nonmetallic dish and set aside while you prepare the sauce.

3 To make the spicy sauce, combine the sieved tomatoes, red wine vinegar, sugar, garlic, dried thyme, dried rosemary, and chili sauce in a bowl until thoroughly blended.

4 Pour the sauce over the pork ribs and toss to coat on all sides. Marinate in the refrigerator for 1 hour.

5 Remove the ribs from the sauce, reserving the sauce for basting. Broil the ribs over hot coals for 5–10 minutes, then move them to a cooler part of the barbecue. Cook for a further 15–20 minutes, turning and basting with the remaining sauce.

6 Transfer the ribs to warm serving plates and garnish with the red chilies (if using). Serve with the mixed salad greens.

COOK'S TIP

For authentic Southern-style ribs make sure you buy pork spareribs and not rib chops. Pork spareribs are often sold cut into individual ribs, but it is quite easy to cut between the ribs with a sharp knife if you cannot obtain them already separated.

Ham & Pineapple Kabobs

Makes 4

INGREDIENTS

1 pound thick ham steak	Gouda, chilled	1/2 tsp ground nutmeg
15 ounce can pineapple	2 tbsp sunflower oil	1/4 tsp ground cloves
chunks, in natural juice	1 clove garlic, crushed	pepper
8 ounces firm brie, Swiss, or	1 tbsp lemon juice	cooked rice, to serve

1 Cut the ham into even-size chunks.

2 Place the ham in a pan of boiling water and simmer for 5 minutes.

3 Drain the pineapple pieces and reserve 3 tbsp of the juice. Cut the cheese into large chunks.

4 To make the baste, combine the pineapple juice, oil, garlic, lemon juice, nutmeg, cloves, and pepper to taste in a small screw-top jar and shake until well combined. Set aside until required.

5 Remove the ham from the pan with a slotted spoon. Thread the ham chunks onto skewers, alternating with the pineapple pieces and the chunks of cheese.

6 Broil the kabobs over warm coals, turning and basting frequently with the oil and pineapple juice mixture, for 2–4 minutes on each side. Broil the kabobs until the pineapple and ham are hot and the cheese is just beginning to melt. Serve the kabobs on a bed of cooked rice, if desired.

COOK'S TIP

Cook the skewers on the barbecue just long enough to reheat the ham and to warm the pineapple. Take care not to overcook the kabobs or you will end up with a sticky and unappetizing mess—the cheese should only just begin to melt.

Honey-glazed Pork Chops

Serves 4

INGREDIENTS

4 lean pork loin chops
4 tbsp clear honey
1 tbsp dry sherry

4 tbsp orange juice
2 tbsp olive oil
1-inch piece fresh ginger root,
  grated

salt and pepper

1 Season the pork chops with salt and pepper to taste. Set aside while you make the glaze.

2 To make the glaze, place the honey, sherry, orange juice, oil, and ginger in a small pan and heat gently, stirring continuously, until the ingredients are blended.

3 Broil the chops on an oiled rack over hot coals for about 5 minutes on each side.

4 Brush the chops with the glaze and broil for another 2–4 minutes on each side, basting frequently with the glaze.

5 Transfer the chops to warm serving plates and serve hot.

COOK'S TIP

To give the recipe a little more punch, stir 1/2 teaspoon of chili sauce or 1 tablespoon of wholegrain mustard into the basting glaze.

VARIATION

This recipe works equally well with lamb chops and with chicken portions, such as thighs or drumsticks. Broil the meat in exactly the same way as in this recipe, basting frequently with the honey glaze—the result will be just as delicious!

Sausages with Barbecue Sauce

Serves 4

INGREDIENTS

2 tbsp sunflower oil
1 large onion, chopped
2 cloves garlic, chopped
8 ounce can chopped
   tomatoes
1 tbsp Worcestershire sauce

2 tbsp Pickapeppa sauce
2 tbsp light brown sugar
4 tbsp white wine vinegar
$^1/_2$ tsp mild chili powder
$^1/_4$ tsp mustard powder

dash of Tabasco sauce
1 pound sausages
salt and pepper
hot dog buns, to serve

1 To make the sauce, heat the oil in a small pan and sauté the onion and garlic for 4–5 minutes, or until softened and just beginning to brown.

2 Add the tomatoes, Worcestershire sauce, Pickapeppa sauce, sugar, wine vinegar, chili powder, mustard powder, Tabasco sauce, and salt and pepper to taste and bring the mixture to a boil.

3 Reduce the heat and simmer gently for

10–15 minutes, until the sauce begins to thicken slightly. Stir occasionally so that the sauce does not burn and stick to the bottom of the pan. Set the sauce aside and keep warm until required.

4 Broil the sausages over hot coals for 10–15 minutes, turning frequently. Do not prick them with a fork or the juices and fat will run out and cause the barbecue to flare.

5 Put the sausages in the hot dog buns and serve with the barbecue sauce.

COOK'S TIP

German wurst sausages are a good choice, as are English Cumberland sausages, which are also available in a coil (secure the coil with skewers so that it does not unravel as it cooks). Venison sausages have a good, gamey flavor and taste wonderful cooked on the barbecue.

Tangy Pork Tenderloin

Serves 4

INGREDIENTS

14 ounces pork tenderloin
3 tbsp orange marmalade
grated rind and juice of
   1 orange
1 tbsp white wine vinegar
dash of Tabasco sauce
salt and pepper

SAUCE:
1 tbsp olive oil
1 small onion, chopped
1 small green bell pepper,
   seeded and thinly sliced
1 tbsp cornstarch
2/3 cup orange juice

TO SERVE:
cooked rice
mixed salad greens

1 Place a large piece of double-thickness foil in a shallow dish. Put the pork in the center of the foil and season.

2 Heat the marmalade, orange rind and juice, vinegar, and Tabasco sauce in a small pan, stirring until the marmalade melts and the ingredients combine.

3 Pour the mixture over the pork and wrap the meat in foil, making sure that the packet is well sealed so that the juices cannot run out. Place over hot coals and broil for about 25 minutes, turning the packet occasionally.

4 Heat the oil and cook the onion for 2–3 minutes, until softened. Add the bell pepper and cook for 3–4 minutes.

5 Remove the pork from the foil and place on the rack. Pour the cooking juices into the pan containing the sauce.

6 Broil the pork for 10–20 minutes, turning, until cooked through and golden.

7 In a bowl, mix the cornstarch with a little orange juice to form a paste. Add to the sauce with the remaining juices. Cook, stirring, until the sauce thickens.

8 Cut the pork into slices and transfer to plates. Spoon the sauce over the pork and serve.

Pork & Sage Kabobs

Makes 12

INGREDIENTS

1 pound ground pork
1/2 cup fresh bread crumbs
1 small onion, very finely
   chopped
1 tbsp fresh sage, chopped
2 tbsp apple sauce

1/4 tsp ground nutmeg
salt and pepper

BASTE:
3 tbsp olive oil
1 tbsp lemon juice

TO SERVE:
6 small pita breads
mixed salad greens
6 tbsp thick, unsweetened
   yogurt

1 Place the pork in a mixing bowl, together with the bread crumbs, onion, sage, apple sauce, nutmeg, and salt and pepper to taste. Mix until the ingredients are well combined.

2 Using your hands, shape the mixture into small balls, about the size of large marbles, and chill in the refrigerator for at least 30 minutes.

3 Meanwhile, soak 12 small wooden skewers in cold water for at least 30 minutes. Thread the pork and sage meatballs onto the skewers.

4 To make the baste, mix together the oil and lemon juice in a small bowl, whisking with a fork until it is well blended.

5 Broil the kabobs over hot coals for 8–10 minutes, turning and basting frequently with the lemon and oil mixture, until the meat is golden and cooked through.

6 Line the pita breads with the salad greens and spoon some of the yogurt on top. Serve with the kabobs.

VARIATION

Save time by shaping the meat mixture into burgers. Chill for at least 20 minutes, then broil, basting with the oil and lemon mixture for 15 minutes, turning once. Serve on hamburger buns topped with a little applesauce.

Steak & Kidney Kabobs

Makes 4

INGREDIENTS

12 ounces lean steak
2 lamb's kidneys
1 small onion, sliced
1/2 tsp dried rosemary
2/3 cup dark beer

8 button mushrooms
8 bay leaves
4 tbsp sunflower oil

TO SERVE:
cooked rice
cherry tomatoes

1 Using a sharp knife, trim the steak and cut it into even-size pieces.

2 Cut the kidneys in half and remove the skin. Snip out the core and cut each half into half again.

3 Place the steak and kidney pieces in a shallow, nonmetallic dish.

4 Add the onions and rosemary to the dish and pour the beer over. Cover and marinate in the refrigerator for at least 4 hours or overnight.

5 Remove the meat from the marinade, reserving 4 tbsp of the marinade for basting.

6 Thread the steak and kidney pieces onto the skewers, alternating with the mushrooms and the bay leaves.

7 Stir the sunflower oil into the reserved marinade. Broil the kabobs over hot coals for 8–10 minutes, turning and basting with the reserved marinade. Take care not to overcook the kidneys or

they will become toughen and become inedible.

8 Serve the kabobs on a bed of cooked rice and with a few cherry tomatoes.

COOK'S TIP

To save time, prepare and marinate the kabobs a day in advance. Place them in a shallow dish and add the marinade. Turn the kabobs occasionally to make sure that they are coated.

Mixed Broil Skewers

Serves 4

INGREDIENTS

8 ounces lamb fillet	BASTE:	TO SERVE:
4 lamb's kidneys	4 tbsp olive oil	4 flat mushrooms
4 thick sausages	2 tbsp lemon juice	2 beefsteak tomatoes
8 slices bacon	1 tbsp fresh mixed herbs, chopped	

1 Cut the lamb fillet into even-size pieces. Skin and core the kidneys and cut each kidney into 4 pieces.

2 Twist the sausages in the center and cut each sausage in half.

3 Stretch out the bacon slices with the back of a knife.

4 Either wrap the bacon around the sausages or simply roll up the slices on their own. Thread the lamb, sausage, bacon, and kidneys onto skewers.

5 To make the baste, mix together the olive oil, lemon juice, and mixed herbs in a small bowl until well combined and let stand until required.

6 Broil the kabobs over hot coals, turning and basting frequently, for 8–10 minutes.

7 Cut the tomatoes and mushrooms into large chunks and then thread them onto separate skewers. Broil the skewers next to the meat for 5 minutes, turning and basting frequently.

8 Transfer the meat skewers to serving plates and serve hot with the tomato and mushroom skewers.

COOK'S TIP

All the elements of this dish can be cooked directly on the barbecue. However, threading them onto skewers makes them quicker and less effort to turn and baste.

Liver & Onion Kabobs

Makes 4

INGREDIENTS

12 ounces lamb's liver
2 tbsp seasoned all-purpose
  flour
1/2 tsp dried mixed herbs
4 1/2 ounces bacon

2 medium onions
6 tbsp butter
2 tsp balsamic vinegar

TO SERVE:
mixed salad greens
tomato quarters

1 Using a sharp knife, cut the liver into bite-size pieces. Mix the flour with the dried herbs and toss the liver in the seasoned flour.

2 Stretch out the bacon slices with the back of a knife. Cut each slice in half and wrap the bacon around half of the liver pieces.

3 Thread the plain liver pieces onto skewers, alternating with the bacon-wrapped liver pieces.

4 Cut the onions into rings and thread over the kabobs. Finely chop the onion rings that are too small to thread over the kabobs.

5 Heat the butter in a small pan and sauté the chopped onions for about 5 minutes, until softened. Stir in the vinegar.

6 Brush the butter mixture over the kabobs and broil over hot coals for 8–10 minutes, basting occasionally with the butter mixture, until

the liver is just cooked, but is still a little pink inside.

7 Transfer the kabobs to serving plates. Serve with mixed salad greens and tomatoes.

COOK'S TIP

Choose thick slices of liver to give good-sized pieces. Use bacon to hold 2–3 pieces of thinner liver together if necessary.

Vegetables & Salads

Vegetarians need never feel left out, as many vegetables cook well on the barbecue, and they taste delicious. Try the Colorful Vegetable Kabobs, the Nutty Rice Burgers, the Vegetarian Sausages, or the delicious Marinated Bean Curd Kabobs. Cook vegetables whole, sliced on skewers, or in packets for main dishes or as tasty side dishes.

Keep your diners happy while they wait for the main course with some tasty nibbles, such as Crispy Potato Skins, Garlic Bread, or Mediterranean Bruschetta, while Stuffed Mushrooms and Stuffed Tomatoes make ideal starters for your vegetarian guests.

If you need inspiration for salads to accompany your barbecued food, look no further. All the salads in this chapter go well with barbecued dishes, and many make ideal starters. Pear & Roquefort Salad and Artichoke & Prosciutto Salad are stylish starters that can be prepared well in advance.

Marinated Bean Curd Skewers

Serves 4

INGREDIENTS

12 ounces bean curd
1 red bell pepper
1 yellow bell pepper
2 zucchini
8 button mushrooms

slices of lemon, to garnish

MARINADE:
grated rind and juice of
$\frac{1}{2}$ lemon

1 clove garlic, crushed
$\frac{1}{2}$ tsp fresh rosemary,
chopped
$\frac{1}{2}$ tsp chopped, fresh thyme
1 tbsp walnut oil

1 To make the marinade, combine the lemon rind and juice, garlic, rosemary, thyme, and oil in a shallow dish.

2 Drain the bean curd, pat it dry on paper towels, and cut it into squares. Add to the marinade and toss to coat. Marinate for 20–30 minutes.

3 Meanwhile, seed and cut the bell peppers into 1-inch pieces. Blanch in boiling water for 4 minutes, rinse in cold water, and drain.

4 Using a canelle knife or potato peeler, remove strips of peel from the zucchini. Cut the zucchini into 1-inch chunks.

5 Remove the bean curd from the marinade, reserving the liquid for basting. Thread the bean curd onto 8 skewers, alternating with the bell pepper pieces, zucchini chunks, and button mushrooms.

6 Broil the skewers over medium hot coals for about 6 minutes, turning

and basting frequently with the marinade.

7 Transfer the skewers to warm serving plates, garnish with slices of lemon, and serve immediately.

VARIATION

For a spicy kabob, make a marinade by mixing together 1 tablespoon of curry paste, 2 tablespoons of oil and the juice of $\frac{1}{2}$ lemon.

Crispy Potato Skins

Serves 4-6

INGREDIENTS

8 small baking potatoes,
   scrubbed
4 tbsp butter, melted
salt and pepper

OPTIONAL TOPPING:
6 scallions, sliced
$\frac{1}{2}$ cup grated Swiss cheese

1$\frac{3}{4}$ ounces salami, cut into
   thin strips

1 Preheat the oven to 400°F. Prick the potatoes with a fork and bake for 1 hour, or until tender. Alternatively, cook in a microwave on High for 12–15 minutes.

2 Cut the potatoes in half and scoop out the flesh, leaving about ¼ inch potato flesh lining the skin.

3 Brush the insides of the potato with melted butter.

4 Place the skins, cut side down, over medium hot coals and broil

for 10–15 minutes. Turn the potato skins over and broil for a further 5 minutes or until they are crispy. Take care that they do not burn.

5 Season the potato skins with salt and pepper to taste, transfer to serving plates and serve while they are still warm.

6 The skins can be filled with a variety of different toppings. Broil the potato skins as above for about 10 minutes, then turn cut side up and sprinkle with slices of

scallion, grated cheese, and chopped salami. Broil for a further 5 minutes until the cheese just begins to melt. Serve the crispy potato skins hot.

COOK'S TIP

Potato skins can be served on their own, but they are delicious served with a dip. Try a spicy tomato or hummus dip.

Spicy Sweet Potato Slices

Serves 4

INGREDIENTS

1 pound sweet potatoes
2 tbsp sunflower oil

1 tsp chili sauce

salt and pepper

1 Bring a large pan of water to a boil, add the sweet potatoes, and parboil them for 10 minutes. Drain the sweet potatoes thoroughly and transfer to a chopping board.

2 Peel the sweet potatoes and cut them into thick slices.

3 Mix the oil, chili sauce, and salt and pepper to taste in a bowl.

4 Brush the spicy mixture over one side of the potatoes. Place the potatoes, oil side down, over medium hot coals and broil for 5–6 minutes.

5 Lightly brush the tops of the potatoes with the oil, turn them over, and broil for a further 5 minutes, or until crisp and golden.

6 Transfer the potatoes to a warm serving dish and serve at once.

COOK'S TIP

Although it is a vegetable, the sweet potato is used in both sweet and savory dishes. It is very versatile and can be boiled, roasted, fried, or cooked, as here, over a barbecue.

VARIATION

For a simple spicy dip combine 2/3 cup sour cream with 1/2 teaspoon of sugar, 1/2 teaspoon of Dijon mustard, and salt and pepper to taste. Chill in the refrigerator until required.

Barbecued Garlic Potato Wedges

Serves 4

INGREDIENTS

3 large baking potatoes, scrubbed
4 tbsp olive oil
2 tbsp butter

2 garlic cloves, chopped
1 tbsp chopped, fresh rosemary
1 tbsp chopped, fresh parsley

1 tbsp chopped, fresh thyme
salt and pepper

1 Bring a large pan of water to a boil, add the potatoes, and parboil them for 10 minutes. Drain the potatoes, rinse under cold water, and drain them again thoroughly.

2 Transfer the potatoes to a chopping board. When the potatoes are cold enough to handle, cut them into thick wedges, but do not remove the skins.

3 Heat the oil and butter in a small pan, together with the garlic. Cook gently until the garlic begins to brown, then remove the pan from the heat.

4 Stir the rosemary, parsley, thyme and salt and pepper to taste into the mixture in the pan.

5 Brush the herb mixture all over the potatoes.

6 Broil the potatoes over hot coals for 10–15 minutes, brushing liberally with any of the remaining herb and butter mixture, or until the potatoes are just tender and cooked through.

7 Transfer to a warm serving plate and serve as a starter or as a side dish.

COOK'S TIP

You may find it easier to barbecue these potatoes in a hinged rack or in a specially designed barbecue roasting tray.

Vegetarian Sausages

Makes 8

INGREDIENTS

1 tbsp sunflower oil
1 small onion, finely chopped
3/4 cup finely chopped
 mushrooms
1/2 red bell pepper, seeded and
 finely chopped

14 ounce can cannolini beans,
 rinsed and drained
1 2/3 cups fresh bread crumbs
1 cup grated cheddar cheese
1 tsp dried mixed herbs
1 egg yolk
seasoned all-purpose flour

oil, to baste

TO SERVE:
rolls
slices of fried onion

1 Heat the oil in a saucepan and sauté the prepared onion, mushrooms, and bell peppers until softened.

2 Mash the cannolini beans in a large mixing bowl. Add the onion, mushroom, and bell pepper mixture, the bread crumbs, cheese, herbs, and egg yolk, and mix together well.

3 Press the mixture together with your fingers and shape into 8 sausages.

4 Roll each sausage in the seasoned flour to coat well. Chill in the refrigerator for at least 30 minutes.

5 Broil the sausages on a sheet of oiled foil set over medium coals for 15–20 minutes, turning and basting frequently with oil, until golden.

6 Split a roll down the middle and insert a layer of fried onions. Place the sausage in the roll and serve.

COOK'S TIP

Take care not to break the sausages when you are turning them over. If you have a hinged rack, oil this and place the sausages inside, turning and oiling frequently.

Nutty Rice Burgers

Makes 6

INGREDIENTS

1 tbsp sunflower oil	2 tbsp Pickapeppa sauce	TO SERVE:
1 small onion, finely chopped	dash of Tabasco sauce	6 sesame seed buns
1 1/2 cups finely chopped	salt and pepper	slices of onion
mushrooms	oil, to baste	slices of tomato
8 cups cooked brown rice	6 individual cheese slices	salad greens
1 2/3 cups bread crumbs	(optional)	
3/4 cup walnuts, chopped		
1 egg		

1 Heat the oil in a pan and sauté the onions for 3–4 minutes, until they just begin to soften. Add the mushrooms and cook for 2 minutes longer.

2 Remove the pan from the heat and mix the rice, bread crumbs, walnuts, egg, and sauces into the vegetables. Season with salt and pepper and mix well.

3 Shape the mixture into 6 burgers, pressing the mixture together with your fingers. Chill in the refrigerator for at least 30 minutes.

4 Broil the burgers on an oiled rack over medium coals for 5–6 minutes on each side, turning once and frequently basting with oil.

5 If desired, top the burgers with a slice of cheese 2 minutes before the end of the cooking time. Broil the onion and tomato slices.

6 Toast the sesame seed rolls at the side of the barbecue. Serve the burgers in the rolls, together with the barbecued onions and tomatoes.

Eggplant & Mozzarella Sandwiches

Serves 2

INGREDIENTS

1 large eggplant
1 tbsp lemon juice
3 tbsp olive oil
1 cup grated mozzarella
   cheese

2 sun-dried tomatoes,
   chopped
salt and pepper

TO SERVE:
Italian bread
mixed salad greens
slices of tomato

1 Slice the eggplant into thin rounds.

2 Mix the lemon juice and olive oil in a small bowl until well combined and season the mixture with salt and pepper to taste.

3 Brush the eggplant slices with the oil and lemon juice mixture and broil over medium hot coals for 2–3 minutes, without turning, until golden on the underside.

4 Turn half of the eggplant slices over and sprinkle with cheese and chopped sun-dried tomatoes.

5 Place the remaining eggplant slices on top of the cheese and tomatoes, turning them so that the pale side is uppermost.

6 Broil for 1–2 minutes, then carefully turn the whole sandwich over, and broil for 1–2 minutes. Baste with the oil mixture.

7 Serve with Italian bread, mixed salad greens, and a few slices of tomato.

VARIATION

Try feta cheese instead of mozzarella but omit the salt from the basting oil. A creamy goat cheese would be equally delicious.

Charbroiled Eggplant

Serves 4

INGREDIENTS

1 large eggplant
3 tbsp olive oil
1 tsp sesame oil
salt and pepper

PESTO:
1 clove garlic
1/4 cup pine nuts
1/4 cup fresh basil leaves
2 tbsp Parmesan cheese
6 tbsp olive oil
salt and pepper

CUCUMBER SAUCE:
2/3 cup unsweetened yogurt
2-inch piece cucumber
1/2 tsp mint sauce

1 Remove the stalk from the eggplant, then cut it lengthwise into 8 thin slices.

2 Lay the eggplant slices on a plate or board and sprinkle them liberally with salt to remove the bitter juices. Set aside until required.

3 Meanwhile, prepare the baste. Combine the olive and sesame oils, season with pepper, and set aside.

4 To make the pesto, put the garlic, pine nuts, basil, and cheese in a food processor until finely chopped. With the machine running, gradually add the oil in a thin stream. Season to taste.

5 To make the minty cucumber sauce, place the yogurt in a mixing bowl. Remove the seeds from the cucumber and dice the flesh finely. Stir into the yogurt with the mint sauce.

6 Rinse the eggplant slices and pat them dry on absorbent paper towels. Baste with the oil mixture and broil over hot coals for about 10 minutes, turning once. The eggplant should be golden and tender.

7 Transfer the eggplant slices to warm individual serving plates and serve immediately with either the cucumber sauce or the pesto.

Stuffed Tomatoes

Makes 8

INGREDIENTS

4 beefsteak tomatoes
4¹/2 cups cooked rice
8 scallions, chopped
3 tbsp chopped, fresh mint
2 tbsp chopped, fresh parsley

3 tbsp pine nuts
3 tbsp raisins
2 tsp olive oil
salt and pepper

---

1 Cut the tomatoes in half, then scoop out the seeds, and discard.

2 Stand the tomatoes upside down on absorbent paper towels for a few moments in order to allow all of the juices to drain out.

3 Turn the tomatoes upright and sprinkle the insides with salt and pepper to taste.

4 Mix together the rice, scallions, mint, parsley, pine nuts, and raisins.

Spoon the mixture into the tomato cups.

5 Drizzle a little olive oil over the tomatoes, then broil them on an oiled rack over medium hot coals for about 10 minutes until they are tender.

6 Transfer the tomatoes to warm serving plates and serve immediately.

COOK'S TIP

Tomatoes are a popular barbecue vegetable and can be quickly cooked. Try broiling slices of beefsteak tomato and slices of onion brushed with a little oil and topped with sprigs of fresh herbs. In addition, cherry tomatoes can be threaded onto skewers and broiled for 5–10 minutes until hot.

Colorful Vegetable Kabobs

Serves 4

INGREDIENTS

1 red bell pepper, seeded	8 cherry tomatoes	SEASONED OIL:
1 yellow bell pepper, seeded	3¹/₂ ounces mushrooms	6 tbsp olive oil
1 green bell pepper, seeded		1 clove garlic, crushed
1 small onion		¹/₂ tsp mixed dried herbs or
		herbes de Provence

1 Cut the bell peppers into 1-inch pieces.

2 Peel the onion and cut it into wedges, leaving the root end just intact to help keep the wedges together.

3 Thread the bell peppers, onion wedges, tomatoes, and mushrooms onto skewers, alternating the colors of the bell peppers.

4 To make the seasoned oil, mix together the oil, garlic, and herbs in a small bowl until well combined. Brush the mixture liberally over the kabobs until well coated.

5 Broil the kabobs over medium hot coals for 10–15 minutes, brushing the vegetables with more of the seasoned oil and turning the skewers frequently.

6 Transfer the vegetable kabobs to warm individual serving plates. Serve with walnut sauce (see Cook's Tip), if you wish.

COOK'S TIP

These kabobs are delicious when accompanied with a walnut sauce. To make the sauce, process 1 cup walnuts in a food processor until they form a smooth paste. With the machine running, add ²/₃ cup heavy cream and 1 tablespoon of olive oil. Season to taste. Alternatively, finely chop the walnuts, then pound them in a mortar with a pestle to form a paste. Mix with the cream and oil, and season.

Charbroiled Mixed Vegetables

Serves 4–6

INGREDIENTS

8 baby eggplant	1 tsp balsamic vinegar, to	BASTE:
4 zucchini	serve	6 tbsp butter
2 red onions		2 tsp walnut oil
4 tomatoes		2 cloves garlic, chopped
salt and pepper		4 tbsp dry white wine or cider

1 To prepare the vegetables, cut the eggplant in half. Trim and cut the zucchini in half lengthwise. Thickly slice the onion and halve the tomatoes.

2 Season all of the vegetables with salt and black pepper to taste.

3 To make the baste, melt the butter with the oil in a saucepan. Add the garlic and cook gently for 1–2 minutes. Remove the pan from the heat and stir in the wine or cider.

4 Add the vegetables to the pan and toss them in the baste mixture. You may need to do this in several batches to ensure that all of the vegetables are coated evenly with the baste mixture.

5 Remove the vegetables from the baste mixture, reserving any excess baste. Place the vegetables on an oiled rack over medium hot coals. Broil for 15–20 minutes, basting with the reserved baste mixture and turning once or twice during cooking.

6 Transfer the vegetables to warm serving plates and serve sprinkled with balsamic vinegar.

COOK'S TIP

Use a long-handled brush for basting food on the barbecue.

Stuffed Mushrooms

Makes 12

INGREDIENTS

12 open-cap mushrooms
4 scallions, chopped
4 tsp olive oil

2 cups fresh brown bread
  crumbs
1 tsp fresh oregano, chopped

3¹/₂ ounces feta cheese or
  chorizo sausage

1 Remove the stalks from the mushrooms and chop the stalks finely.

2 Sauté the mushroom stalks and scallions in half of the oil.

3 Transfer the mushroom stalks and scallions to a large mixing bowl. Add the bread crumbs and oregano to the mushrooms and scallions, mix, and set aside.

4 If using feta cheese, crumble the cheese into small pieces in a small bowl, using a fork or your fingers.

5 If you are using chorizo sausage, remove the skin and chop the flesh finely.

6 Add the cheese or chorizo to the breadcrumb mixture and mix well.

7 Spoon the stuffing mixture into the mushroom caps. Carefully drizzle the oil over the mushrooms. Broil on an oiled rack over medium hot coals for 8–10 minutes. Transfer the mushrooms to serving plates and serve hot.

COOK'S TIP

If only small mushrooms are available, place a sheet of oiled foil on top of the barbecue rack and cook the mushrooms on this. This will stop the mushrooms from cooking too quickly and burning, and will stop any excess stuffing from dropping onto the coals.

Corn Cobs

Serves 4

INGREDIENTS

4 corn cobs, with husks	1 tsp chopped, fresh chives	salt and pepper
8 tbsp butter	1 tsp chopped, fresh thyme	
1 tbsp chopped, fresh parsley	rind of 1 lemon, grated	

1 To prepare the corn cobs, peel back the husks and remove the silken hairs.

2 Fold back the husks and secure them in place with string if necessary.

3 Blanch the corn cobs in a large saucepan of boiling water for about 5 minutes, in batches if necessary. Remove the cobs with a slotted spoon and drain thoroughly.

4 Broil the cobs over medium hot coals for 20–30 minutes, turning them frequently.

5 Meanwhile, soften the butter and beat in the parsley, chives, thyme, lemon rind, and salt and pepper to taste.

6 Transfer the corn cobs to serving plates, remove the string and pull back the husks. Serve with a generous portion of herb butter.

COOK'S TIP

When you are buying fresh corn, look for plump, tightly packed kernels. If you are unable to get fresh cobs, cook frozen corn cobs on the barbecue. Spread some of the herb butter onto a sheet of double thickness foil. Wrap the cobs in the foil and broil among the coals for about 20–30 minutes.

Pumpkin Packets with Chili & Lime

Serves 4

INGREDIENTS

1 pound 9 ounces pumpkin or squash	2 tbsp butter	2 tsp lime juice
2 tbsp sunflower oil	1/2 tsp chili sauce	
	rind of 1 lime, grated	

1 Halve the pumpkin or squash and scoop out the seeds. Rinse the seeds and reserve. Cut the pumpkin into thin wedges and peel.

2 Heat the oil and butter together in a large pan, stirring continuously until melted. Stir in the chili sauce, lime rind, and juice.

3 Add the pumpkin or squash and seeds to the pan and toss to coat in the flavored butter.

4 Divide the mixture among 4 double-thickness sheets of foil.

Fold the foil to enclose the pumpkin or squash mixture completely.

5 Cook the foil packets over hot coals for 15–25 minutes, or until the pumpkin or squash is cooked through and tender.

6 Transfer the packets to warm serving plates. Open the packets at the table and serve at once.

VARIATION

Add 2 teaspoons of curry paste to the oil instead of the lime and chili.

COOK'S TIP

It is a good idea to wear disposable gloves when slicing and seeding chilies. Alternatively, rub a little oil over your fingers—the oil will help to prevent your skin from absorbing the chili juice. Wash your hands thoroughly afterward.

Garlic Bread

Serves 6

INGREDIENTS

³/₄ cup butter, softened 3 cloves garlic, crushed	2 tbsp chopped, fresh parsley pepper	1 large or 2 small loaves of French bread

1 Mix together the butter, garlic, and parsley in a bowl until well combined. Season to taste with pepper and mix until well combined.

2 Cut the French bread into thick slices.

3 Spread the flavored butter over one side of each slice and reassemble the loaf on a large sheet of thick foil.

4 Wrap the bread well and cook over hot coals for 10–15 minutes, until the garlic butter melts and the bread is piping hot.

5 Serve as an accompaniment to a wide range of dishes.

COOK'S TIP

Some recipes suggest that you do not cut all the way through the bread when you slice it, but you will find it a lot easier to serve if you do. Simply keep the slices in order and reassemble once buttered.

VARIATION

For a tasty variation, sprinkle a little grated mozzarella cheese between each slice of bread. Reassemble the loaf and cook for 10–15 minutes, until the cheese has just melted

COOK'S TIP

When garlic is cooked like this on a barbecue, the sweetness of it comes to the fore. Garlic combines well with fresh, crusty white bread and the result tastes delicious.

Mediterranean Bruschetta

Serves 4

INGREDIENTS

1 Italian loaf or small loaf of French bread	1 plump clove garlic extra virgin olive oil	freshly grated Parmesan cheese, (optional)

1 Slice the bread in half crosswise and again lengthwise to give 4 portions.

2 Do not peel the garlic clove, but cut it in half using a sharp knife.

3 Broil the bread over hot coals for a few minutes on both sides until golden brown.

4 Rub the garlic, cut side down, all over the toasted surface of the bread.

5 Drizzle the olive oil over the bread and serve hot as an accompaniment.

6 If using Parmesan cheese, sprinkle the cheese over the bread. Return the bread to the barbecue, cut side up, for 1–2 minutes, until the cheese just begins to melt. Serve hot.

VARIATION

For a tasty appetizer, serve the bruschetta topped with chopped tomatoes mixed with a few chopped anchovies or olives.

COOK'S TIP

As ready-grated Parmesan quickly loses its pungency and "bite," it is better to buy small quantities of the cheese in one piece and grate it yourself as needed. Tightly wrapped in plastic wrap or foil, it will keep in the refrigerator for several months. Grate it just before using, for maximum flavor.

COOK'S TIP

If you do not peel the garlic, the smell will not transfer to your fingers.

Caesar Salad

Serves 6-8

INGREDIENTS

2 thick slices of white bread
2 tbsp sunflower oil
2 slices fatty bacon, or 6
  chopped anchovies

1 clove garlic
1³/₄ ounces Parmesan cheese
1 large romaine lettuce

DRESSING:
1 small egg
juice 1 lemon
6 tbsp olive oil
salt and white pepper

1 To make the croutons, remove the crusts from the bread and discard. Cut the bread into small cubes. Heat the sunflower oil in a skillet and fry the bread cubes until a golden brown color. Drain the bread cubes thoroughly on absorbent paper towels.

2 Chop the slices of bacon and fry until crisp. Drain on absorbent paper towels.

3 Cut the garlic in half and rub all around the inside of a serving dish. This will give the salad just a hint of garlic.

4 Wash the lettuce, tear into bite-size pieces, and place in the serving dish.

5 Using a vegetable peeler, shave peelings off the cheese.

6 To make the dressing, whisk the egg in a small bowl. Gradually whisk in the lemon juice and oil. Season with salt and pepper to taste.

7 Pour the salad dressing over the lettuce and toss to coat. Serve sprinkled with the croutons, bacon or anchovies, and Parmesan.

COOK'S TIP

Pregnant women, children, and people with weak immune systems may wish to avoid eating recipes containing raw egg.

Coleslaw

Serves 10–12

INGREDIENTS

²/₃ cup mayonnaise
²/₃ cup low-fat unsweetened
    yogurt
dash of Tabasco sauce

1 medium head white cabbage
4 carrots
1 green bell pepper
2 tbsp sunflower seeds

salt and pepper

1 To make the dressing, combine the mayonnaise, yogurt, Tabasco sauce, and salt and pepper to taste in a small bowl. Leave to chill in the refrigerator until required.

2 Cut the cabbage in half and then into quarters. Remove and discard the tough center stalk. Shred the cabbage leaves finely. Wash the leaves and dry them thoroughly.

3 Peel the carrot and shred in a food processor. Alternatively, coarsely grate the carrot.

4 Quarter and seed the bell pepper and cut the flesh into thin strips.

5 Combine the vegetables in a large serving bowl and toss to mix. Pour the dressing on and toss until the vegetables are well coated. Let chill.

6 Just before serving, place the sunflower seeds on a cookie sheet and toast in the oven or under the broiler until golden.

7 Scatter the sesame seeds over the coleslaw and serve.

COOK'S TIP

You can make coleslaw a few days in advance. To ensure that the sunflower seeds are crispy, add them just before serving.

VARIATION

For a slightly different taste, add one or more of the following ingredients to the coleslaw: raisins, grapes, grated apple, chopped walnuts, cubes of cheese, or roasted peanuts.

Green Bean & Carrot Salad

Serves 4

INGREDIENTS

12 ounces green beans	DRESSING:	salt and pepper
8 ounces carrots	2 tbsp extra virgin olive oil	
1 red bell pepper	1 tbsp red wine vinegar	
1 red onion	2 tsp sun-dried tomato paste	
	$^1/_4$ tsp superfine sugar	

1 Top and tail the beans and blanch them in boiling water for 4 minutes, until just tender. Drain the beans and rinse them under cold water until they are cool. Drain the beans again thoroughly.

2 Transfer the beans to a large salad bowl.

3 Peel the carrots and cut them into matchsticks.

4 Halve and seed the bell pepper and cut the flesh into thin strips.

5 Peel the onion and cut it into thin slices.

6 Add the carrot, bell pepper, and onion to the beans and toss to mix.

7 To make the dressing, place the oil, wine vinegar, sun-dried tomato paste, sugar, and salt and pepper to taste in a small screw-top jar and shake well.

8 Pour the dressing over the vegetables and serve or chill in the refrigerator until required.

COOK'S TIP

Use canned beans if fresh ones are unavailable. Rinse off the salty liquid and drain well. There is no need to blanch canned beans.

Spinach & Orange Salad

Serves 4-6

INGREDIENTS

8 ounces baby spinach leaves
2 large oranges
1/2 red onion

DRESSING:
3 tbsp extra virgin olive oil
2 tbsp freshly squeezed
    orange juice
2 tsp lemon juice

1 tsp clear honey
1/2 tsp wholegrain mustard
salt and pepper

1 Wash the spinach leaves under cold running water and then dry them thoroughly on absorbent paper towels. Remove any tough stalks and tear the larger leaves into smaller pieces.

2 Slice the top and bottom off each orange with a sharp knife, then remove the peel.

3 Carefully slice between the membranes of the orange to remove the individual segments.

4 Using a sharp knife, finely chop the onion.

5 Mix together the spinach leaves and orange segments and arrange in a serving dish. Scatter the chopped onion over the salad.

6 To make the dressing, whisk together the olive oil, orange juice, lemon juice, honey, mustard, and salt and pepper to taste.

7 Pour the dressing over the salad just before serving. Toss the salad well to coat the leaves.

COOK'S TIP

Tear the spinach leaves into bite-size pieces rather than cutting them because cutting bruises the leaves.

VARIATION

Use a mixture of spinach and watercress leaves, if you prefer a slightly more peppery flavor.

Potato Salad

Serves 4

INGREDIENTS

1 pound 9 ounces tiny new potatoes	1 tsp paprika	TO GARNISH:
8 scallions	salt and pepper	2 tbsp snipped chives
1 hard-boiled egg (optional)		pinch of paprika
generous 1 cup mayonnaise		

1 Bring a large pan of lightly salted water to a boil. Add the potatoes to the pan and cook for 10–15 minutes, or until they are just tender.

2 Drain the potatoes in a colander and rinse them under cold running water until they are completely cold. Drain them again thoroughly. Transfer the potatoes to a mixing bowl and set aside until required.

3 Using a sharp knife, trim and slice the scallions thinly on the diagonal.

4 Shell and chop the hard-boiled egg.

5 Combine the mayonnaise, paprika, and salt and pepper to taste in a bowl. Pour the mixture over the potatoes.

6 Add the scallions and egg (if using) to the potatoes and toss together.

7 Transfer the potato salad to a serving bowl, sprinkle with snipped chives and a pinch of paprika. Cover and chill in the refrigerator until required.

VARIATION

To make a lighter dressing, use a mixture of half mayonnaise and half unsweetened yogurt.

VARIATION

Add cubes of cheese to the potato salad, if liked.

Tabouleh

Serves 4

INGREDIENTS

1 1/2 cups cracked wheat
8 ounces tomatoes
1 small onion
1/4 cucumber
1/2 red bell pepper

4 tbsp chopped, fresh parsley
3 tbsp chopped, fresh mint
2 tbsp pine nuts
4 tbsp lemon juice
4 tbsp extra virgin olive oil

2 cloves garlic, crushed
salt and pepper

1 Place the cracked wheat in a large bowl and cover with plenty of boiling water. Let stand for about 30 minutes, or until the grains are tender and have swelled in size.

2 Drain the wheat through a large strainer. Press down with a plate in order to remove as much water as possible. Transfer the wheat to a large mixing bowl.

3 Cut the tomatoes in half, scoop out the seeds, and discard them.

Chop the flesh into fine dice. Using a sharp knife, finely chop the onion.

4 Scoop out the seeds from the cucumber and discard them. Finely dice the cucumber flesh.

5 Seed the bell peppers and chop the flesh. Add the prepared vegetables to the wheat, with the herbs and pine nuts. Toss until mixed.

6 Mix together the lemon juice oil, garlic, and salt and pepper to taste.

7 Pour the mixture over the wheat and vegetables and toss together. Chill in the refrigerator until required.

COOK'S TIP

This salad is best made a few hours before it is required to allow time for the flavors to develop and blend together. It can even be made a few days ahead, if wished.

Hot Lentil Salad with Balsamic Dressing

Serves 6-8

INGREDIENTS

³/4 cup Puy lentils, cooked
4 tbsp olive oil
1 small onion, sliced
4 stalks celery, sliced
2 cloves garlic, crushed
2 zucchini, trimmed and diced

4¹/2 ounces green beans,
  trimmed and cut into short
  lengths
¹/2 red bell pepper, seeded and
  diced
¹/2 yellow bell pepper, seeded
  and diced

1 tsp Dijon mustard
1 tbsp balsamic vinegar
salt and pepper

---

1 Place the lentils in a large mixing or serving bowl. The lentils can still be warm, if wished.

2 Heat the oil in a saucepan and sauté the onion and celery for 2–3 minutes, until softened but not browned.

3 Add the garlic, zucchini, and green beans to the pan and cook for 2 minutes, stirring.

4 Add the bell peppers to the pan and cook for 1 minute.

5 Stir the mustard and the balsamic vinegar into the pan and mix until warm and thoroughly combined.

6 Pour the warm mixture over the lentils and toss together to mix well. Season with salt and pepper and serve immediately.

COOK'S TIP

To cook the lentils, rinse them well and place in a large saucepan. Cover with plenty of cold water and bring to a boil. Boil rapidly for 10 minutes, then reduce the heat, and simmer for 35 minutes, until the lentils are tender. Drain well.

Italian Mozzarella Salad

Serves 6

INGREDIENTS

7 ounces baby spinach leaves

4 1/2 ounces watercress

4 1/2 ounces mozzarella cheese

8 ounces cherry tomatoes

2 tsp balsamic vinegar

1 1/2 tbsp extra virgin olive oil

salt and freshly ground black pepper

1 Wash the spinach and watercress and drain thoroughly on absorbent paper towels. Remove any tough stalks. Place the spinach and watercress leaves in a serving dish.

2 Cut the mozzarella cheese into small pieces and scatter them over the spinach and watercress leaves.

3 Cut the cherry tomatoes in half and scatter them over the salad.

4 Sprinkle with the balsamic vinegar and oil, and season with salt and pepper to taste. Toss the mixture together to coat the leaves. Serve at once or chill in the refrigerator until required.

VARIATION

Include feta or halloumi cheese instead of mozzarella for a change, and use sherry vinegar instead of balsamic vinegar, if preferred.

COOK'S TIP

Mozzarella is a highly popular cheese. It is a soft, fresh cheese with a piquant flavor, traditionally made from water buffalo's milk. It is usually sold surrounded by whey to keep it moist. Buffalo milk is now scarce, and so nowadays this cheese is often made with cow's milk. Mozzarella combines well with tomatoes, and this combination is now a classic.

Artichoke & Prosciutto Salad

Serves 4

INGREDIENTS

9¹/₂ ounce can artichoke
    hearts in oil, drained
4 small tomatoes
¹/₂ cup sun-dried tomatoes in
    oil
1¹/₂ ounces prosciutto

¹/₂ cup pitted black olives,
    halved
few basil leaves

DRESSING:
3 tbsp olive oil
1 tbsp white wine vinegar

1 clove garlic, crushed
¹/₂ tsp mild mustard
1 tsp clear honey
salt and pepper

1 Make sure the artichoke hearts are thoroughly drained, then cut them into quarters, and place in a bowl.

2 Cut each fresh tomato into wedges. Slice the sun-dried tomatoes into thin strips. Cut the prosciutto into thin strips and add to the bowl containing the artichokes together with the tomatoes and olive halves.

3 Keeping a few basil leaves whole for garnishing, tear the remainder of the leaves into small pieces and add to the bowl containing the other salad ingredients.

4 Put the oil, wine vinegar, garlic, mustard, honey, and salt and pepper to taste in a screw-top jar and shake vigorously until well blended.

5 Pour the dressing over the salad and toss.

6 Serve the salad garnished with a few whole basil leaves.

COOK'S TIP

Use bottled artichokes in oil as they have a better flavor. Rinse canned artichokes to remove the salty liquid.

Pear & Roquefort Salad

Serves 4

INGREDIENTS

1 3/4 ounces Roquefort cheese	few leaves of lollo rosso	pepper
2/3 cup low-fat unsweetened yogurt	few leaves of radiccio	whole chives, to garnish
2 tbsp snipped chives	few leaves of corn salad	
	2 ripe pears	

1 Place the cheese in a bowl and mash with a fork. Gradually blend the yogurt into the cheese to make a smooth dressing. Add the snipped chives and season with pepper according to taste.

2 Tear the lollo rosso, radiccio, and corn salad leaves into manageable pieces. Arrange the salad greens on a serving platter or on individual serving plates.

3 Quarter and core the pears, and then cut them into slices.

4 Arrange the pear slices over the salad greens.

5 Drizzle the dressing over the pears and garnish with a few whole chives. Serve at once.

COOK'S TIP

Arrange the Pear & Roquefort Salad on individual plates for an attractive starter, or on one large serving platter for a side salad.

COOK'S TIP

Look for bags of mixed salad greens, as these are generally more economical than buying lots of different greens separately. If you are using greens that have not been prewashed, rinse them well and dry them thoroughly on absorbent paper towels or in a salad spinner. Alternatively, wrap the greens in a clean dish cloth and shake dry.

Pasta Salad with Basil Vinaigrette

Serves 4

INGREDIENTS

2 cups fusilli (pasta spirals)
4 tomatoes
$^1/_3$ cup black olives
$^1/_2$ cup sun-dried tomatoes in
  oil
2 tbsp pine nuts

2 tbsp grated Parmesan
  cheese
fresh basil, to garnish

VINAIGRETTE:
$^1/_4$ cup basil leaves
1 clove garlic

2 tbsp grated Parmesan
  cheese
4 tbsp extra virgin olive oil
2 tbsp lemon juice
salt and pepper

1 Cook the pasta in lightly salted boiling water for 10–12 minutes, until just tender, or according to the instructions on the packet. Drain the pasta, rinse under cold water, then drain again thoroughly. Place the pasta in a large bowl.

2 To make the vinaigrette, place the basil leaves, garlic, cheese, oil, and lemon juice in a food processor. Season

with salt and pepper to taste. Process until the leaves are well chopped and the ingredients are combined. Alternatively, finely chop the basil leaves by hand and combine with the other vinaigrette ingredients. Pour the vinaigrette over the pasta and toss to coat.

3 Cut the tomatoes into wedges. Pit and halve the olives. Slice the sun-dried tomatoes. Toast the pine nuts on a cookie sheet

under the broiler until golden brown.

4 Add the tomatoes (fresh and sun-dried) and the olives to the pasta and mix until combined.

5 Transfer the pasta to a serving dish, scatter over the Parmesan and pine nuts, and garnish with a few basil leaves.

Mango & Wild Rice Salad

Serves 6

INGREDIENTS

1/2 cup wild rice	1/4 cup ready-to-eat dried	sprigs of fresh cilantro or
1 cup Basmati rice	apricots, chopped	mint, to garnish
3 tbsp hazelnut oil	3/4 cup slivered almonds	
1 tbsp sherry vinegar	2 tbsp chopped, fresh cilantro	
1 ripe mango	or mint	
3 stalks celery	salt and pepper	

1 Cook the rice in separate pans in lightly salted boiling water. Cook the wild rice for 45–50 minutes, and the Basmati rice for 10–12 minutes. Drain, rinse, and drain again. Put the rice in a bowl.

2 Mix the oil, vinegar, and seasoning together. Pour the mixture over the rice and toss well.

3 Cut the mango in half lengthwise, as close to the pit as possible. Remove and discard the pit.

4 Peel the skin from the mango and cut the flesh into slices.

5 Slice the celery thinly and add to the cooled rice with the mango, apricots, almonds, and chopped herbs. Toss together and transfer to a serving dish. Garnish with sprigs of fresh herbs.

COOK'S TIP

To toast almonds, place them on a cookie sheet in a preheated oven at 350°F for 5–10 minutes. Alternatively, toast them under the broiler, turning frequently and keeping a close eye on them because they will quickly burn.

Mixed Bean Salad

Serves 6-8

INGREDIENTS

14 ounce can small navy
    beans, drained
14 ounce can red kidney
    beans, drained
14 ounce can dried lima
    beans, drained

1 small red onion, thinly sliced
6 ounces green beans, topped
    and tailed
1 red bell pepper, halved and
    seeded

DRESSING:
4 tbsp olive oil
2 tbsp sherry vinegar
2 tbsp lemon juice
1 tsp light brown sugar
1 tsp chili sauce (optional)

1 Put the canned beans in a large mixing bowl. Add the sliced onion and mix together.

2 Cut the green beans in half and cook in lightly salted boiling water for about 8 minutes, until just tender. Rinse under cold water and drain again. Add to the mixed beans and onions.

3 Place the bell pepper halves, cut side down, on a broiler rack and cook until the skin blackens and chars. Cool slightly, then put them into a plastic bag for about 10 minutes. Peel away the skin from the bell peppers and discard. Roughly chop the bell pepper flesh and add it to the beans.

4 To make the dressing, place the oil, sherry vinegar, lemon juice, sugar, and chili sauce (if using) in a screw-top jar and shake vigorously.

5 Pour the dressing over the mixed bean salad and toss well. Chill in the refrigerator until required.

VARIATION

You can use any combination of beans in this salad. For a distinctive flavor, add 1 teaspoon of curry paste instead of the chili sauce.

Mediterranean Bell Pepper Salad

Serves 4

INGREDIENTS

2 red bell peppers, halved and
  seeded
2 yellow bell peppers, halved
  and seeded
3 tbsp extra virgin olive oil

1 onion, cut into wedges
2 large zucchini, sliced
2 garlic cloves, sliced
1 tbsp balsamic vinegar

1³/₄ ounces anchovy fillets,
  chopped
¹/₄ cup pitted black olives,
  quartered
fresh basil leaves

1 Place the bell pepper halves, cut side down, on a broiler pan and cook until the skin blackens and chars. Cool slightly, then put them into a plastic bag for about 10 minutes.

2 Peel away the skin from the bell peppers and discard. Cut the flesh into thick strips.

3 Heat the oil in a large skillet, add the onion, and sauté gently for 10 minutes, or until softened. Add the zucchini slices, garlic, and bell pepper strips to the skillet and cook, stirring occasionally, for another 10 minutes.

4 Add the vinegar, anchovies, and olives to the pan. Season to taste. Mix well and let cool.

5 Reserve a few basil leaves for garnishing, then tear the remainder into small pieces. Stir them into the salad.

6 Transfer the bell pepper salad to a serving dish and garnish with a few fresh, whole basil leaves.

COOK'S TIP

Balsamic vinegar is made in and around Modena in Italy. Its rich, mellow flavor is perfect for Mediterranean-style salads, but if it is unavailable, use sherry vinegar or white wine vinegar instead.

Desserts

Don't forget the dessert—it can be cooked on the barbecue, too. Although desserts are not the most important part of a barbecue spread, they are always fun to cook and most can be prepared in advance and left above the cooling coals to cook to perfection while you dig into the main course.

Fruit is always a good choice because it contrasts so well with the often rich and filling main courses. Try croissants filled with chocolate and raspberries or panettone topped with marscapone cheese.

Have plenty of ice cream as a standby. It's popular with the children and is delicious served with barbecued fruits on a hot summer day. Thick, unsweetened yogurt or light cream are also ideal accompaniments. If you don't want a hot dessert, prepare a simple fruit salad.

For a quick sweet treat thread marshmallows onto skewers and hold them above the warm coals until just softened.

Barbecued Baked Apples

Serves 4

INGREDIENTS

4 medium cooking apples
1/4 cup chopped walnuts
1/4 cup ground almonds
2 tablespoons light brown
   sugar

1/4 cup chopped cherries
2 tbsp preserved ginger,
   chopped
1 tbsp amaretto (almond-
   flavored liqueur) (optional)

4 tbsp butter
heavy cream or unsweetened
   yogurt, to serve

1 Core the apples and using a knife, score each one around the middle to prevent the apple skins from splitting during cooking.

2 To make the filling, mix together the walnuts, almonds, sugar, cherries, ginger, and amaretto, if using, in a small bowl.

3 Spoon the filling mixture into each apple, pushing it down into the hollowed-out core. Mound a little of the filling mixture on top of each apple.

4 Place each apple on a large square of double-thickness foil and generously dot all over with the butter. Wrap up the foil so that the apple is completely enclosed.

5 Cook the foil packets containing the apples over hot coals for 25–30 minutes, or until tender.

6 Transfer the apples to warm, individual serving plates. Serve with plenty of whipped heavy cream or thick unsweetened yogurt.

COOK'S TIP

If the coals are dying down, place the foil packets directly onto the coals, raking them up around the apples. Cook for 25–30 minutes and serve with the cream or yogurt.

Fruity Skewers with Chocolate Dipping Sauce

Serves 4

INGREDIENTS

selection of fruit (choose from oranges, bananas, strawberries, pineapple chunks (fresh or canned), apricots (fresh or canned), eating apples, pears, kiwi fruit)	1 tbsp lemon juice CHOCOLATE SAUCE: 4 tbsp butter 4 squares dark chocolate, broken into small cubes ¹/₂ tbsp cocoa powder	2 tbsp corn syrup BASTE: 4 tbsp clear honey grated rind and juice of ¹/₂ orange

1 To make the chocolate sauce, place the butter, chocolate, cocoa powder, and corn syrup in a small pan. Heat gently at the side of the barbecue, stirring continuously, until all of the ingredients have melted and are well combined.

2 To prepare the fruit, peel and core if necessary, then cut into large, bite-size pieces or wedges as appropriate. Dip apples, pears, and bananas in lemon juice to prevent discoloration. Thread the pieces of fruit onto skewers.

3 To make the baste, mix together the honey, orange juice and rind, heat gently if required, and brush over the fruit.

4 Broil the fruit skewers over warm coals for 5–10 minutes, until hot. Serve with the chocolate dipping sauce.

COOK'S TIP

If the coals are too hot, raise the rack so that it is about 6 inches above the coals or spread out the coals a little to reduce the heat. Do not assemble the fruit skewers more than 1–2 hours before they are required.

Toffee Fruit Kabobs

Serves 4

INGREDIENTS

2 eating apples, cored and cut
    into wedges
2 firm pears, cored and cut
    into wedges
juice of $^1/_2$ lemon

2 tbsp light brown sugar
$^1/_4$ tsp ground allspice
2 tbsp unsalted butter, melted

SAUCE:
9 tbsp butter
$^1/_2$ cup light brown sugar
6 tbsp heavy cream

1 Toss the apple and pears in the lemon juice to prevent any discoloration.

2 Mix the sugar and allspice together and sprinkle over the fruit.

3 Carefully thread the fruit pieces onto skewers.

4 To make the toffee sauce, place the butter and sugar in a saucepan and heat, stirring gently, until the butter has melted and the sugar has dissolved.

5 Add the cream to the saucepan and bring to a boil. Boil for 1–2 minutes, then set aside to cool slightly.

6 Meanwhile, place the fruit kabobs over hot coals and broil for about 5 minutes, turning and basting frequently with the melted butter, until the fruit is just tender.

7 Transfer the fruit kabobs to warm serving plates and serve with the slightly cooled toffee sauce.

COOK'S TIP

Firm apples that will keep their shape are needed for this dish—varieties such as Golden Delicious, Granny Smith and Braeburn are a good choice. Soft apples and pears will become mushy as they cook.

VARIATION

Sprinkle the fruit kabobs with chopped walnuts or pecans before serving, if you wish.

Chocolate & Raspberry Croissants

Serves 4

INGREDIENTS

4 butter croissants

4 tsp raspberry preserve

6 squares dark chocolate

3/4 cup raspberries

oil, for greasing

1 Slice the croissants in half. Spread the bottom half of each croissant with 1 teaspoon of the raspberry preserve.

2 Grate or finely chop the chocolate and sprinkle over the preserve.

3 Lightly grease 4 sheets of foil, brushing with a little oil.

4 Divide the raspberries equally among the croissants and replace the top half of each croissant. Place each croissant onto a sheet of foil, wrapping the foil around the croissant to enclose it completely.

5 Place the rack 6 inches above hot coals. Transfer the croissants to the rack and leave them to heat through for 10–15 minutes, or until the chocolate just begins to melt.

6 Remove the foil and transfer the croissants to individual serving plates. Serve hot.

VARIATION

You could also use milk chocolate or a mixture of milk and dark chocolate for this dish.

VARIATION

For a delicious chocolate and strawberry filling for the croissants, use sliced strawberries and strawberry preserve instead of the raspberries.

COOK'S TIP

Use the best quality fruit preserve you can find. Better still, use homemade jellies and preserves.

Baked Bananas

Serves 4

INGREDIENTS

4 bananas	ORANGE-FLAVORED CREAM:
2 passion fruit	$^2/_3$ cup heavy cream
4 tbsp orange juice	3 tbsp confectioners' sugar
4 tbsp orange-flavored liqueur	2 tbsp orange-flavored liqueur

1 Peel the bananas and place each one onto a sheet of foil.

2 Cut the passion fruit in half and squeeze the juice of each half over each banana. Spoon the orange juice and liqueur over each banana.

3 Fold the kitchen foil over the top of the bananas to enclose them.

4 Cook the bananas over hot coals for about 10 minutes, or until they are warm and just tender.

5 To make the orange-flavored cream, pour the heavy cream into a mixing bowl and sprinkle with the confectioners' sugar. Whisk the mixture until it is standing in soft peaks. Carefully fold in the orange-flavored liqueur and chill in the refrigerator until required.

6 Transfer the foil packets containing the bananas to warm, individual serving plates. Open the foil packets at the table and then serve the bananas immediately together with the orange-flavored cream.

VARIATION

Leave the bananas in their skins for a really quick dessert. Split the banana skins and put in 1–2 squares of chocolate. Wrap the bananas in foil and barbecue for 10 minutes, or until the chocolate just melts.

Panettone with Mascarpone & Strawberries

Serves 4

INGREDIENTS

2 cups strawberries	6 tbsp Marsala wine	4 slices panettone
1/4 cup superfine sugar	1/2 tsp ground cinnamon	4 tbsp mascarpone cheese

1 Hull and slice the strawberries and place them in a bowl. Add the sugar, Marsala, and cinnamon to the strawberries.

2 Toss the strawberries in the sugar and cinnamon mixture until they are well coated. Chill in the refrigerator for at least 30 minutes.

3 When ready to serve, transfer the slices of panettone to a rack set over medium hot coals. Broil the panettone for about

1 minute on each side, or until golden brown.

4 Remove the panettone from the barbecue and transfer to serving plates. Top the panettone with the mascarpone cheese and the marinated strawberries. Serve immediately.

VARIATION

Spread mascarpone cheese onto sweet biscuits that have been toasted on the barbecue.

COOK'S TIP

Mascarpone is an Italian soft cheese with a rich, creamy texture, tasting like very thick cream. It will melt into the panettone, making it quite delicious. If mascarpone is unavailable, cream cheese or ricotta would be good alternatives.

Piña Colada Pineapple

Serves 4

INGREDIENTS

1 small pineapple
4 tbsp unsalted butter
2 tbsp light brown sugar
²/₃ cup grated fresh coconut

2 tbsp coconut-flavored
   liqueur or rum

1 Using a very sharp knife, cut the pineapple into quarters and then remove the tough core from the center, leaving the leaves attached.

2 Carefully cut the pineapple flesh away from the skin. Make horizontal cuts across the flesh of the pineapple quarters.

3 Place the butter in a pan and heat gently until melted, stirring continuously. Brush the melted butter over the pineapple and sprinkle with the sugar.

4 Cover the pineapple leaves with kitchen foil to prevent them from burning, and transfer them to a rack set over hot coals.

5 Broil the pineapple for about 10 minutes.

6 Sprinkle the coconut over the pineapple and broil, cut side up, for 5–10 minutes, or until the pineapple is piping hot.

7 Transfer the pineapple to serving plates and remove the foil from the leaves. Spoon a little coconut-flavored liqueur or rum over the pineapple and serve at once.

COOK'S TIP

Fresh coconut has the best flavor for this dish. If you prefer, however, you can use shredded coconut.

Stuffed Pears with Mincemeat

Serves 4

INGREDIENTS

4 firm pears	5 tbsp cake crumbs or 4	1 tbsp butter
1 tsp lemon juice	amaretti cookies, crushed	ice cream, to serve
2 tbsp mincemeat		

1 Using a sharp knife, cut the pears in half. Using a teaspoon, scoop out the core and discard.

2 Brush the cut surface of each of the pear halves with a little lemon juice to prevent discoloration.

3 Mix together the mincemeat and cake crumbs, or crushed amaretti cookies.

4 Divide the mixture among the pear halves, spooning it into a mound where the core has been removed.

5 Place 2 pear halves on a large square of double-thickness foil and generously dot all over with the butter.

6 Wrap up the foil around the pears so that they are completely enclosed.

7 Transfer the foil packets to a rack set over hot coals. Cook for 25–30 minutes, or until the pears are hot and just tender.

8 Transfer the pears to individual serving plates. Serve with 2 scoops of ice cream per serving.

VARIATION

Use mincemeat to stuff apples instead of pears, and bake them on the barbecue in the same way.

COOK'S TIP

If the coals are dying down, place the foil packets directly onto the coals and barbecue for 25–30 minutes.

Peaches with Creamy Mascarpone Filling

Serves 4

INGREDIENTS

4 peaches
1 cup mascarpone cheese

¹/₂ cup pecan or walnuts,
  chopped

1 tsp sunflower oil
4 tbsp maple syrup

1 Cut the peaches in half and remove the pits. If you are preparing this recipe in advance, press the peach halves together again and wrap them in plastic wrap until required.

2 Mix the mascarpone and pecan or walnuts together in a small bowl until well combined. Chill in the refrigerator until required.

3 To serve, brush the peaches with a little oil and place on a rack set over medium hot coals. Broil the peach halves for 5–10 minutes, turning once, until they are hot.

4 Transfer the peach halves to a serving dish and top with the mascarpone and nut mixture.

5 Drizzle the maple syrup over the peaches and mascarpone filling, and serve at once.

COOK'S TIP

Mascarpone cheese is high in fat; you can use thick unsweetened yogurt.

VARIATION

You can use nectarines instead of peaches for this recipe, if you prefer. Remember to choose ripe, but fairly firm, fruit which won't go soft and mushy when it is barbecued. Prepare the nectarines in the same way as the peaches and barbecue for 5–10 minutes.

Exotic Fruity Packets

Serves 4

INGREDIENTS

1 papaya	1 tbsp grenadine	light cream or unsweetened
1 mango	3 tbsp orange juice	yogurt, to serve
1 star fruit		

1 Cut the papaya in half, scoop out the seeds with a spoon, and then discard the seeds. Peel the papaya and cut the flesh into thick slices.

2 Prepare the mango by cutting it lengthwise in half either side of the central pit.

3 Score each mango half in a criss-cross pattern. Push each mango half inside out to separate the cubes and cut them away from the peel.

4 Using a sharp knife, slice the star fruit.

5 Place all of the fruit in a bowl and mix them together.

6 Mix the grenadine and orange juice together and pour over the fruit. Marinate for at least 30 minutes.

7 Divide the fruit among 4 double-thickness squares of foil and gather up the edges to form a packet that encloses the fruit.

8 Place the foil packet on a rack set over warm coals and barbecue the fruit for 15–20 minutes.

9 Serve the fruit in the packet, with light cream or yogurt.

COOK'S TIP

Grenadine is a sweet syrup made from pomegranates. If you prefer, you could use pomegranate juice instead of the grenadine for this recipe. To extract the juice, cut the pomegranate in half and squeeze gently with a lemon squeezer—do not press too hard or the juice may become bitter.